The Great Gardens of Cornwall:
The People and their Plants

Tim Hubbard

with a foreword by
Alan Titchmarsh

THE
GREAT
GARDENS
OF CORNWALL

Alison Hodge

Published in 2017 by
Alison Hodge
1a Gwavas Road, Newlyn, Penzance, Cornwall TR18 5LZ
info@alison-hodge.co.uk
www.alisonhodgepublishers.co.uk

Cover design: Christopher Laughton

ISBN 13 978 0 906720 98 1

British Library Cataloguing-in-Publication Data
A catalogue record for this book is available from
the British Library.

Title page: Tremenheere Sculpture Gardens.

Printed in China.

Contents

Foreword – Alan Titchmarsh

MBE VMH DL

Television presenter, author, and gardener

'I wish I could grow that'…

Facing page:
Telopea speciosissima *at Tremenheere Sculpture Gardens.*

Gardeners are not, by nature, jealous souls, but every now and then they gaze, green with envy, upon another's plants and think, 'I wish I could grow that.' It is something that happens to me in Cornwall more than anywhere else in the country. Spring comes early to this western extremity of England, and milder temperatures mean that a far wider range of plants can be grown than in most mainland gardens. The Curator of Abbey Garden, Tresco, Mike Nelhams, and I have a standing joke: he says that he has the best job in the world and that I have the second best. I say it is the other way round, but we both know what we mean – to be involved with gardens and gardening is the best thing in life, and to be involved with a garden in or near to Cornwall takes some beating. I manage to get down there at least every other year, and my gardens on the Isle of Wight and in Hampshire are richer as a result, for I cannot resist a pot or two of this or that just to see if it will grow 'back home'. My island garden is especially mild and goes some way towards ameliorating my envy of Cornish gardens.

My memories of them are fond and numerous: of the great canyon of hydrangeas and gunnera at Trebah, of drowning in rhododendrons at Caerhays, and marvelling at camellias in the woodlands at Antony – a favourite garden with one of the best viewpoints in the British Isles, gazing out over the Tamar with Devon on one side and Cornwall on the other. The Eden Project has been a tremendous success – and no wonder, for it can enchant all the family, adults and children alike – with its spectacular biomes that bring the rainforest to the UK. There is history to be admired at Lanhydrock, and history to be unearthed at The Lost Gardens of Heligan – an entrancing story that never fails to inspire. The list goes on, and so, thank goodness, do the Cornish gardens and those who look after them. As always, I look forward eagerly to my next visit and my next armful of plants that will bring a little bit of Cornwall home with me. Without their magic, our lives would be all the poorer.

Introduction –
Charles Williams,

Chairman, The Great Gardens of Cornwall

Twenty-five years ago, a distinguished group of garden owners and managers met on Tresco to inaugurate The Great Gardens of Cornwall. Then, as now, over seventy gardens in Cornwall regularly opened to the public, but the then Cornwall County Council was obliged to give them all equal amounts of taxpayer-funded publicity. This had forced the larger and better-known gardens to undertake their own independent marketing initiatives. The obvious answer was to combine into a new, and then unique, gardens group, guaranteeing visitors excellent and varied gardens in wonderful Cornish settings. It has been said many times over the last twenty-five years that if The Great Gardens of Cornwall had not been created, the best gardens in Cornwall would never have become the outstanding collective visitor experience they are today. The combined strengths arising from our co-operation and joint marketing ensure that our unique gardens are now a key feature of the Cornish tourist scene all year round. Over two million visitors each year to our nineteen separate gardens speaks for itself.

Many people ask what makes a Cornish garden 'great'. A few of our great Cornish gardens are indeed quite small, or relatively new, and so less well known. Others have long been of national significance for their historic plant collections, unique microclimates, amazing restorations, or the successes of European and Lottery funding. What all have in common is, first, excellence – which is why we market them together in our own inimitable way. Second, visitor facilities including catering, shops, car-parking, facilities for people with disabilities, and toilets. Third, we all work together in amicable co-operation to ensure that Cornwall offers garden-lovers an exceptional garden holiday, no matter when in the year they visit.

I should like to thank all those Great Gardens members, their head gardeners and friends who have worked so hard to write and produce this excellent book, which is testament to our joint achievements and successes over the last twenty-five years.

Do come and experience the diversity and welcome of all our amazing great Cornish gardens for yourselves.

The Great Gardens of Cornwall …

What do they mean to you?

'The great gardens of Cornwall are plant-rich and timeless in their appeal. Since my first visit in October 1963 I have been tempted back most every year, and every season has its floral pleasures, old favourites and new arrivals jostling for attention. Boring never, revitalizing ever!'

Roy Lancaster CBE, VMH, FI Hort, FLS
Plantsman, gardener, author and broadcaster

'Irrespective of the time of year, whenever I explore Cornish gardens, I'm always amazed by their diversity of location and setting, and, due to the climate, their rich range of plants whose wealth encourages visitors from around the world. However, for me, spring is THE time when you stand in amongst those magnificent magnolias, in awe of their flowers in shades of pink, white and purple. Seen in their thousands they are indeed one of the wonders of the plant world!'

Jim Gardiner
Executive Vice President and former Director of Horticulture, Royal Horticultural Society

'It is always an honour to visit The Great Gardens of Cornwall. They are a treasure trove of exceptional plants, a living testament to the great plant hunters like Ernest Wilson, George Forrest and Cornishman William Lobb, and a monument to the vision of the landowners who created them.'

Matt Biggs
Gardener, writer and broadcaster

'Cornish gardens offer enormous beauty throughout the year. In spring the fields of the Tamar valley are covered in daffodils for the London markets. In summer the awesome gunneras tower over shady nooks, and in autumn the crocosmia burns bright in the hedges. But my favourite of all is the Padstow Pride scenting the hedgerows and bringing memories of long childhood summers.'

Fern Britton
Television presenter and author

'Cornwall is a long thin slice of horticulture heaven. Its combination of subtropical valley gardens, historic plant collections and rich examples of gardening eccentricity or sheer bravado, along with a wonderful array of proper plantsperson's nurseries and the longest growing season in the country, mean that we obsessive gardeners lucky enough to live here would be quite happy never again to cross the Tamar into England.'

Patrick Gale
Gardening novelist

'I've been visiting Cornish gardens all my life, and I'm still amazed by the variety of plants that grow there; not just the exotics of Tresco or Trebah but the lush inland woodland gardens with their spectacular rhododendrons and camellias. I come back time after time just to wonder at those amazing magnolias.'

Rick Stein
Chef, restaurateur, writer and television presenter

'The spring flush of choice flowering trees and shrubs in Cornish gardens always reminds me of the commitment of the great plant collectors of the past, and the vast dedication from those who care for these spectacular plants in amazing gardens all over the county today. Their joint efforts result in a paradise, not only for the garden and plant lover but also for people who just wish to admire the awakening of spring in this part of the world.'

Christine Walkden
Gardener, horticulturist, writer and broadcaster

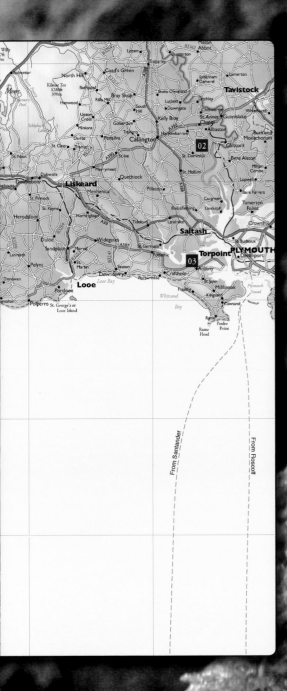

The Great Gardens of Cornwall: Locations

Key

01 Lanhydrock House

02 Cotehele House

03 Antony

04 The Eden Project

05 The Lost Gardens of Heligan

06 Trewithen

07 Caerhays Castle and Gardens

08 Lamorran House Gardens

09 Trelissick Garden

10 Trebah Garden

11 Glendurgan Garden

12 Trengwainton Garden

13 Abbey Garden, Tresco

14 Bonython Estate Gardens

15 Trewidden Garden

16 Godolphin Estate

17 Tregothnan

18 Tremenheere Sculpture Gardens

19 Tregrehan

Abbey Garden, Tresco

Augustus John Smith, who took on the tenancy of the Isles of Scilly in 1834.

Tresco's Abbey Garden is unique, and has been described as the most extraordinary garden in the United Kingdom. Lying some thirty miles out into the Atlantic beyond Land's End, the island of Tresco faces the worst storms imaginable, yet the Abbey Garden grows tender and rare plants from all over the world.

In 1834, the tenancy of the Isles of Scilly was taken by Augustus John Smith, on a ninety-nine-year lease. At that time the islands were impoverished; families struggled to survive by fishing or farming; housing stock was extremely poor, and education and health care virtually non-existent. The new Lord Proprietor had a great deal of work to do. He based his approach on the ideas of the social reformer Jeremy Bentham, and had four goals: educating the island children, stopping smuggling, creating leases that would reward long-term improvement of the land, and abandoning the practice of divided family holdings.

Initially Augustus Smith lived on St Mary's, but the site of the former priory of St Nicholas on Tresco appealed to him. It was connected to the Benedictine Abbey in Tavistock, and had been lived in until the sixteenth century. It had (some) shelter, fresh water and privacy, and he quickly erected walls to the south and west. It was around those walls that the Abbey Garden began. Augustus Smith realized that the mild

Jubaea chilensis, the barrel-trunked Chilean wine palm, is one of thousands of species growing near the old abbey walls.

Scillonian climate would allow plants to grow virtually all year round, so plants were sent to Tresco from the Royal Botanic Gardens, Kew to establish his collection.

However, despite the relatively warm climate, salt-laden winds were a problem. Augustus Smith used the ever-present gorse as an initial shelterbelt, but went on to plant many species of trees to break the wind's force. *Cupressus macrocarpa* (Monterey cypress) and *Pinus radiata* (Monterey pine, formerly *Pinus insignis*) were immediately successful, and formed the structure behind which all future planting would take place. Smith designed three major walks, all running east to west across the garden's slope with a variety of paths connecting them, as well as one major set of steps.

Known as the Neptune Steps, this has been a central feature of the garden ever since.

By this time, Augustus Smith was becoming something of a horticultural expert and had made contact with Sir William Hooker (father of the plant hunter Joseph Hooker) at Kew, and Lord Ilchester at Abbotsbury garden in Dorset. Plants from South Africa, South America, Australia and New Zealand were sent to Tresco, and by 1858 he had completed his grand design. Augustus Smith died in 1872, admired and respected by many Scillonians for his commitment and care, and having laid the foundations for the future success of the garden.

Thomas Algernon Dorrien-Smith, Augustus's nephew, resigned his commission as a Lieutenant in the Tenth Hussars to take on his uncle's role as Lord Proprietor. The economy of Scilly was once again in the doldrums, and Thomas Algernon encouraged the first commercial growing of daffodils for the London flower markets, researching growing techniques on trips to Holland and Belgium. Of all the varieties, 'Soleil d'Or' and 'Paper White' were the most successful – both were early and prolific. The Abbey Garden continued to grow under Thomas Algernon's care, and he lived on Tresco with his wife and seven children for over forty years.

By the time Major Arthur Dorrien-Smith inherited Tresco in 1918, he was already an enthusiastic gardener, having collected plants and seed during his service in South Africa, helped to establish Melbourne's Botanic Garden, and sourced plant material in the Auckland and Campbell islands off New Zealand. Among

The Neptune Steps, a central feature of the garden, were designed by Augustus Smith in the nineteenth century.

Top: Olives, echiums and agaves … Mediterranean-style planting.

Above: Tresco Children, *by sculptor David Wynne.*

the plants he introduced to the UK was *Olearia semidentata*, which flowered on Tresco for the first time in 1913. The financial and economic effect of the First World War meant that Arthur was forced to relinquish his responsibility for the other islands in the group to the Duchy of Cornwall, but he continued as Chairman of the Isles of Scilly Council for the rest of his lifetime.

Tresco's Head Gardener from 1922 was Kew-trained William Andrews. The rarity of the plants and the location of the Abbey had drawn visitors to the garden since Augustus Smith's time, but now numbers increased. Travellers would ring a bell at the Valhalla entrance, and Mr Andrews would escort them around in exchange for a donation to the Tresco Nursing Association.

By 1935, Major Arthur's acquisitions meant that Tresco's plant list stood at 3,500 species and varieties. New arrivals around this time included *Freycinetia banksii, Cyathea medullaris* (the black

tree fern) and *Meryta sinclairii*, which joined sixty-nine species of *Agave*, 159 species of *Pelargonium* and 153 species of *Mesembryanthemum*.

In 1955 Lieutenant Commander Thomas Dorrien-Smith succeeded his father, and it was he who developed the island's economy to embrace tourism as well as agriculture. The garden had been regularly open to the public since 1950 at a charge of 2/6d (12.5 pence), and now it became internationally well known, with Royal visits and exhibits at the Chelsea Flower Show.

The present owner, Robert Dorrien-Smith, took over from his father in 1973. With his then Head Gardener Peter Clough, and later with current Garden Curator Mike Nelhams and Head Gardener Andrew Lawson, he has successfully taken the Abbey Garden into the twenty-first century. Two extremely rare events – snow damage in 1987 and a hurricane in 1990 – brought havoc

Top: Tall hedges of evergreen oak shelter the garden.

Above: Robert Dorrien-Smith.

Top: Tom Leaper's bronze agave-shaped fountain.

Above: Head Gardener Andrew Lawson.

to the garden, and Robert Dorrien-Smith oversaw an extensive replanting scheme and the restoration of the all-important shelterbelt. He took the decision to radically redesign and replant one badly affected area of the garden, and a major new Mediterranean Garden was conceived and constructed. It's planted with olives, rosemary, lavender and cork oaks, along with South African aloes and proteas and Californian ceanothus. It features a spectacular bronze agave-shaped fountain by sculptor Tom Leaper and an open gazebo, decorated with shells and mosaics, by Robert's wife, Lucy Dorrien-Smith.

Today, Tresco is a player on the global horticultural stage. Mike Nelhams, who first came to Tresco as a student in 1976 and became Head Gardener in 1983, lectures on the garden and its plants all around the world. He is an RHS judge on the Tender Plants Committee, escorts horticultural tours and now, as Garden

Curator, has a wider role in the island's operations. For him, *Leucadendron argenteum* (the South African silver tree) sums up Tresco's magic: 'It's the most stunning plant. It loves the thin soil and the sunshine we can offer it on the island and it thrives here, even in the Atlantic gales. To see those silver leaves against a Scillonian blue sky is absolutely magical.'

Five generations of the family and long-serving head gardeners have lived and worked in this extraordinary part of the UK. Tresco's Abbey Garden is a tribute to all of them, and is open all year round.

Top: Lucy Dorrien-Smith decorated the gazebo.

Above: Garden Curator Mike Nelhams.

Bonython Estate Gardens

Top: Sue Nathan.

Above: Miss Lyle (right) and friends in the walled garden.

Bonython Estate Gardens is the only Great Garden of Cornwall on the Lizard peninsula. Most of the Lizard is bleak and windswept, its moors covered in thin scrub and heather but, at Bonython, Richard and Sue Nathan have developed exquisite planting and bold landscapes in a relatively short space of time.

It was the Bonithon family, who claimed descent from Britain's Norman conquerors, who gave their name to the estate, living there from the thirteenth to the early eighteenth century. A succession of owners followed them, including John Trevenen of Helston, who built the Georgian manor house – albeit incorporating parts of the Bonithon building – as well as the present walled garden. The Lyle family, whose wealth came from the boom in tin mining, took over the estate from Trevenen and in the 1830s brought in the famous Treseder nurserymen to establish windbreaks around the property, providing much-needed shelter.

Mary Lucy Lyle, living in New Zealand, inherited the property from her father in 1921 and moved to Cornwall. No plant lover, she declared a policy of 'no flowers or colour in the garden', and was not amused when an acquaintance jokingly 'planted' plastic flowers around the house overnight! She died in 1949 and left the house and

the grounds to her cousin Robert (though a condition of her will was that he change his surname from Wyatt to her own). Later High Sheriff of Cornwall, Robert Lyle attempted various planting schemes – including the colourful flowers of which his benefactor would have disapproved. He also brought plumbing and electricity to the manor, and implemented a schedule of restoration, but when he died in 1989 there was still much work to be done.

Above: The valley of the second lake, carpeted with bluebells and wild garlic in early summer.

Facing page: The first lake, with grasses, canna lilies and other reminders of South Africa.

Sue and Richard Nathan fell in love with an estate agent's photograph of the façade of the manor, but there was little cultivated garden to speak of. The beds in the walled garden had been grassed over, and the orchard had reverted to a paddock. A major casualty of years of neglect were the lakes, rendered virtually invisible by undergrowth and saplings. However, the Nathans recognized that the overall structure was still intact, that the soil was in good heart, and that growing conditions were excellent.

As with many of the Great Gardens, the importance of a shelterbelt to give some respite from Cornwall's coastal gales was uppermost in their minds, and in 1999, within weeks of moving into the manor (which faces head on to the prevailing salty wind), the first of 15,000 new trees was being planted. Many of these have now reached maturity, blending in with the ancient trees from the original Treseder plantings.

Another priority was to clear the dense undergrowth in the valley of the second lake (the second in a series of three). This area of the garden had become virtually impenetrable as bramble, sycamore and scrub had gained control. It took two months simply to clear the site, armed with loppers and chainsaws. Sue remembers,

Top: Camassias beside the stream.

Above: Woodland plantings include tree ferns and azaleas.

'We invited Charles Williams of Burncoose Nurseries to visit and help us decide what trees would grow in this sheltered part of the garden. After removing some ninety stumps and planting twenty-five specimen trees, I felt the area still needed further landscaping.'

With an unerring eye for both colour and design, Sue planted in stages and also recreated a stream flowing from the first lake to the second, using various pieces of granite and stone to line the banks. Camassias and irises bloom here with water flowing from springs on the surrounding moorland, 'Everything from a trickle to a torrent!' laughs Sue, and this now feeds all three lakes.

Sue is from South Africa, and she has been keen to test her favourite plants from home against the rigours of the wet and windy Cornish climate. 'Hot' colours abound, with *Stipa arundinacea*, *Kniphofia*, *Crocosmia* 'Lucifer' and *Leucadendron salignum* 'Fireglow' all doing well. Restios, proteas and canna lilies ('Durban'

is a favourite) have all been planted here and, to many people's surprise, are thriving.

Each of the three lakes in the sequence has distinctive planting. The second – now referred to as 'Lake Sue', and the site of so much early clearance – is today surrounded by bright perennials, while the first, with its grassy banks, is home to an island of towering, shady *Gunnera manicata* (giant rhubarb). The third lake was also choked with undergrowth when the Nathans arrived – so much so that it was only discovered a month after they moved in. The former quarry has been lined with clay, and its surrounding rock faces and banks have woodland plantings of wildflowers, azaleas and rhododendrons, along with plectranthus (members of the mint family), tree ferns and bamboos.

Closer to the manor, Sue has completely redesigned the walled garden. Within it lies a traditional English 'feminine' herbaceous border, box hedging, paths and an ancient stone seat. The swim-

Top: The ancient seat in the walled garden.

Above: Dramatic plantings by the first lake.

ming pool has also been redesigned, and now provides a modern focus with an infinity pool flowing over on four sides. Steps lead to the second part of the garden, which is not only decorative but produces herbs, vegetables and picking flowers for the house. Sue has been careful to use a restricted colour palette here. 'I designed the planting here with a colour theme of pink and burgundy so that most of the flowers, and even the vegetables, are in various shades of only those colours.'

Behind the manor is an intriguing contemporary water feature where a pergola supports a grape vine, surrounded by restios, grasses and bamboos, which form 'walls' to the outdoor living space, with steps leading to a formal chamomile lawn.

Sue is the first to admit that when she left South Africa her horticultural knowledge was limited. 'It's been a steep learning curve,' she says, 'and back-breaking work, but the Cornish climate is just perfect for my plants. I'm not so much interested in their rarity or specialty, but I want species with just the right format and colour to do well in their particular position.' The garden is testament to year upon year of her hard work and eye for detail and colour. The growing yew chapel is now substantial with an altar, crucifix and seats with oak buttresses. In addition, the infinity pool, a reflecting pond in front of the manor, and thyme and alpine terraces all contribute to the richness of Sue's themed colour canvas.

Bonython Estate Gardens is proud of the fact that there is flowering interest for much of the year. Unlike in many Cornish gardens, the spring-flowering magnolias, azaleas and camellias are followed by blue hydrangeas – they line the drive under an avenue of copper beech trees (a legacy of the Lyles) – and then perennials and grasses throughout the summer and into autumn. The thatched summerhouse (used as a tea house) was created from a collapsed stone bothy, and overlooks the apple orchard, stocked with traditional Cornish varieties.

What began as a retirement project for Sue and Richard has become an all-absorbing passion and, with the help of one full-time gardener and additional seasonal help, they have devoted themselves to the estate. Some twenty acres (8 ha) are now planted, and there are plans to develop even more. While the Georgian manor (which Pevsner called 'exceptionally elegant') is essentially a family home, visitors are welcome to the garden from April until September every year. Many are amazed that it is relatively young in Cornish terms. 'It feels as if the garden's been here for ever,' said a visitor. 'The planting seems mature and very much of the place. It's perfect.'

Top: Herbs, flowers and vegetables flourish in the lower garden.

Above: The thatched summerhouse, used as a tea house.

Facing page: The infinity pool and the alpine terrace.

Choosing a camellia in a garden centre or nursery anywhere in the world, many people will turn the label to read the name *'williamsii'*, not realizing its link to Cornwall and Caerhays. If there is one name that is synonymous with Cornish gardens, it is that of Williams. Four successive generations of the family have provided unrivalled continuity (along with only four head gardeners since 1897), and have dedicated themselves to making Caerhays one of the most outstanding gardens in the UK.

The imposing castle, backed by woodland, is close to the shore east of the Roseland peninsula. It was bought in 1854 by Michael Williams, at one time MP for West Cornwall and Chairman of the famous Cornwall Railway. He renovated the building and began to develop its grounds. His grandson, John Charles (J.C.) Williams, was born there in 1861. In his twenties, J.C. developed an interest in horticulture, specifically orchids, and in the 1880s began breeding daffodils. The Caerhays Garden Book begins on 1 January 1897, much of it in J.C.'s own handwriting. We can read of his passion for gardening and for the natural history that surrounded him on the south Cornish coast:

'I saw the first swallow,'
(31 March 1897)

Caerhays Castle and Gardens

A page from The Garden Book, begun in 1897 by J.C. Williams.

'We lately had a terrific easterly gale; it cut the boughs off the yew as if a man had worked with his clipper at it for hours,' (1 February 1917);

and – a comment with which many gardeners would sympathize:

'Rain and slugs are the main crop this season,' (14 November 1924).

Between 1902 and 1932, J.C. Williams sponsored, either personally or as part of syndicates, nine expeditions by the great 'Chinese' plant hunter George Forrest. Rhododendrons became immensely popular in the UK around the time of the First World War and, over the years, Forrest introduced more than 300 new species, including the iconic *Rhododendron sinogrande* (giant Chinese rhododendron). His expeditions – particularly the early ones – were dangerous, and conditions were hard:

> *'Our little band, numbering about eighty, were picked off one by one, or captured, only fourteen escaping. Ten women, wives and daughters of our followers, committed suicide by throwing themselves into the stream. Of my own seventeen collectors and servants, only one escaped.'* (19 July 1905)

J.C. also received seed from Ernest 'Chinese' Wilson, through the famous Veitch nurseries, and he grew them on in excitement and anticipation. The Garden Book records:

> *'Have agreed with Veitch for the right to select 15 of Wilson's rhododendrons, in which there are several yellows.'*

The new plants flourished in the Cornish climate in the care of J.C. and his Head Gardeners John Martin and Charles Michael. *Rhododendron fargesii* flowered here for the first time in Europe in 1911, *R. auriculatum* in 1912 and *R. calophytum* in 1915. The rhododendron called after J.C. (*R. williamsianum*) had been introduced to the UK by Wilson in 1908, and a specimen was awarded the prize for best plant at one of the Rhododendron Society's first shows, in 1926.

It wasn't just rhododendrons that captivated J.C. Williams. The gardens at Caerhays were now home to a huge variety of plants from the UK and all around the world that thrived in the lush, temperate climate of the south coast, sheltered from the prevailing winds by judicious windbreak planting. But one plant, more than any other, was to secure Caerhays' place in horticultural history. The now world-famous *Camellia williamsii* had unremarkable beginnings. On a mountainside in China, George Forrest had found a plant of what would later become *Camellia saluenensis*:

Above: Ernest 'Chinese' Wilson.

Facing page: Rhododendron sinogrande, *and plant hunter George Forrest on his pony,* c. 1905, Dali, Yunnan, China.

Above: Camellia saluenensis.

Facing page: Charles H. Williams (top) and Head Gardener Jamie Parsons.

'17686 Thea speciosa, Pitard form. A1311. Volcanic mountain, north west of Tenyyuch. Lat 25, 10N. Altitude 8,000 ft. [2,440 m.]. Evergreen shrub of 6–12 ft. [2–4 m.]. Flowers rose pink. Stony hillside.' (February 1918)

Now at home at Caerhays, the first flowering of *Camellia speciosa* (soon to be renamed *C. saluenensis*) was noticed (some may say slightly grudgingly) by J.C. on 7 January 1922:

'Some Camellias are nice, speciosa particularly.'

The following year, J.C.'s stroke of genius was to cross *Camellia saluenensis* with *C. japonica*, thereby producing a strong new strain of camellia that created huge excitement. Unlike the japonica strain, the new *C. williamsii* were extremely floriferous; they were easy to grow, and the new blooms were shed by the plant after they had flowered. In addition, and to many people's surprise, they survived Cornish winters outside with no protection. An evergreen plant with strong winter colour, that could grow well in most temperate climates; nurseries couldn't grow them fast enough to cope with demand.

J.C. Williams died in 1939 (fittingly, sitting in his beloved garden, looking out to sea), and was succeeded by Charles Williams. Charles, too was a keen gardener and hybridizer, although heavily involved in wartime politics. An apocryphal story tells that the garden may have become overrun

by brambles and neglect had he not spent all his spare time with a scythe!

The present owner of Caerhays, and Chair of The Great Gardens of Cornwall, Charles H. Williams, takes up the story:

> 'My father, F. Julian Williams, who took on the mantle of running Caerhays in 1955, was not initially a gardener. His self-taught knowledge from reference books however soon became considerable and my brother and I were brought up in the garden.'

In the twenty-first century, Charles Williams is very much continuing his ancestors' commitment to the gardens at Caerhays, working with Head Gardener Jaimie Parsons. Caerhays holds the National Collection of Magnoliaceae, with over 100 species and more than 500 named varieties from all around the world, as well as a National Collection of Podocarpus and many rare evergreen oaks and Lithocarpus.

Locally born, Jaimie first came to the estate when he was only eight years old, on shooting parties with his father,

Above: Magnolia *'Bishop Peter'*.

Facing page: Rhododendron *'Ostara' flowering in the woods above the castle.*

though he says his love of gardening came from his grandfather and great-grandfather. After school he embarked on a two-year Youth Training Scheme, spending time at the then Probus Demonstration Garden, Camborne College, and the well-known Watering Lane Nursery near St Austell. He went on to train at Cannington College in Bridgwater, and became a self-employed horticulturist working for, among others, Burncoose Nurseries. In April 1994 he joined the gardening team at Caerhays, and two years later, on the retirement of Philip Tregunna as Head Gardener, Jaimie succeeded him. 'I was lucky,' he says. 'Philip and I got on well and, after he'd officially left, he'd come down to the glass houses from time to time and spend hours with me passing on his extraordinary horticultural knowledge… and even one or two secrets.'

The gardens open each year from mid-February to early June, when the magnolias and camellias for which it is world-renowned, along with other spring flowers, are at their best. Modern technology helps people stay in touch with the estate throughout the year. The Garden Book, so diligently handwritten by J.C. Williams, has been digitized, and internet users can read regular comments about planting schemes, new additions and flowering dates. Burncoose Nurseries near Redruth (a regular Gold Medal winner at Chelsea Flower Show) is the retail arm of the estate. Its online catalogue makes it one of the largest plant mail order businesses in the UK. Times have changed since the days of the Victorian plant hunters and, in the light of the international Nagoya Protocol which, among other things, attempts to control indiscriminate plant imports and exports, Burncoose maintains licences and contacts which allow Caerhays to source extraordinary new plants, continuing the old traditions.

The Eden Project

Above: Tim Smit in the Eden Project's Rainforest Biome.

Facing page: Dahlias bloom in the Outdoor Gardens.

The Eden Project – the so-called 'eighth wonder of the world' – is a global phenomenon. It has already attracted over 18 million visitors and contributed £1.7 billion pounds to the local economy.

The story of the Eden Project is inextricably linked to the development of The Lost Gardens of Heligan. While Tim Smit (now Sir Tim Smit KBE) was restoring Heligan, he realized that the human stories associated with plants were sometimes more interesting to the general visitor than the plants themselves. Along with Heligan's Horticultural Director, Philip McMillan Browse, and Trustee Peter Thoday, he began a search to find a site in which these stories could be told. A conservatory in Heligan's Flower Garden was considered, as was a half-glazed area within the Dairy Quarry.

By May 1994, the concept had developed into a series of glasshouses or polytunnels, linked at the centre, each focusing on the plants from a different climatic area of the world. Gradually, the scale of what was being considered grew and grew, and Tim and his team decided that the site they were looking for would have to be not only very special, but also within reach of Cornwall's main trunk road, the A30, to attract the maximum number of visitors.

Then, driving on that same road, alongside the then landscape of dis-

used china clay pits and spoil heaps, the setting sun lit not only the abandoned workings, but also an idea in Tim's mind that the location they were looking for was right on their doorstep. 'It was the strangest thing. The instant my eyes fell on Bodelva Pit, I knew it was the one, exactly as it was meant to be,' he says.

The scale of the plan was enormous. With an energetic team behind him, Tim involved funders, corporations, planners, architects, horticulturists and designers undaunted by the prospect of developing an exhausted, steep-sided former clay pit. To many it

In the Rainforest Biome, tropical plants now flourish. Visitors enjoy the Canopy Walkway (facing page), and an authentic south-east Asian home and vegetable garden (above left).

was an unlikely location: some sixty metres deep and the area of thirty-five football pitches, with no soil and fifteen metres below the water table.

In time, the idea formed that the site should reflect three of the world's climatic zones. A 'roofless' area would grow plants thriving in Cornwall's temperate zone – native flora and familiar crops, as well as plants from elsewhere in the world. A 'humid tropics' zone would be home to a lush, wet, hot jungle with plants from West Africa, the Amazon and South East Asia, and a 'warm temperate' zone would grow plants from the Mediterranean, South Africa and California.

The first task was to refill the pit with the spoil that had been dumped around its perimeter, and the first dumper truck set to work on 15 October 1998. Nearly two million tonnes of earth had to be moved; by the time the trucks had finished, the pit's floor had been raised by around twenty metres and the sides lowered by thirteen metres. The scale of the project was becoming clear.

The design of the now-famous biomes – interconnecting spheres of hexagons and pentagons, built on the principles of geodesic domes – was approved. Architects Nicholas Grimshaw & Partners, landscape architects led by Dominic Cole, engineers Anthony Hunt Associates, and MERO UK plc – the specialists who would clad the giant shapes – began their groundbreaking work. Scaffolding sixty metres high and using 100,000 poles, grew up where the biomes were to stand, and the structure began to take shape, with the lightweight metal frames covered in a high-tech transparent foil, generally known as ETFE.

Meanwhile, plans for the plants and the soils within the biomes were also taking shape. There was no topsoil within the pit. For environmental and financial reasons, taking it from elsewhere was ruled out, and the horticultural team set about making 85,000 tonnes of it – enough to cover the site to a depth of some 700 mm.

The Mediterranean Biome recreates landscapes of southern Europe, South Africa and California. Bacchanalian sculptures revel in the vineyard.

The well-known Watering Lane Nursery, five miles away, had been purchased already and, by the time the site was ready to receive them, it contained 80,000 plants. Other original plantings came from Cambridge Botanic Garden, Wageningen University in the Netherlands, and the government of the Seychelles. Planting began on 25 September 2000, with large cranes working within the biomes to manoeuvre the larger specimens.

In early 2001 the biomes were opened in a low-key ceremony attended by just the Eden team, contractors and the Bishop of Truro. The official opening on 17 March by contrast attracted the attention of the world's media, and visitors (some half million of whom had already witnessed part of the construction process wearing hard hats and hi-vis jackets while riding on a land train) poured in.

Since Eden's early days the site, and the plants, have matured. The Rainforest Biome now houses towering palms and bamboos (the tree canopy is almost fifty metres high); the Mediterranean Biome has seen seasons of crops come and go, and the outdoor area has established displays of spring bulbs, landscaped crops and mature shrubs alongside new plantings. In 2016, over 2,000 plants of one hundred varieties of *Kniphofia* (Red-hot Poker) were planted amid *Trachycarpus fortunei* (Chusan palms) as part of the 'Bright Sparks' project. Horticultural highlights in the Rainforest Biome include the decorative

Aristolochia cathcartii (Dutchman's Pipe), which produces flowers with cream-coloured, purple-veined, pipe-like structures; *Amorphophallus titanum* (the Titan arum) – one of the largest flowering structures in the plant kingdom – and crops such as *Theobroma cacao* (cocoa), from which chocolate is produced.

The Eden Project is an educational charity. In September 2005 a new building – The Core – was opened as a base for teaching and learning alongside the biomes. Every year, some 47,000 children come in groups (as well as those who come with their families) to explore for themselves, and to discover the role plants play in our lives.

A huge team of horticulturists, teachers, engineers, artists and scientists creates experiences for the thousands of visitors each year who come to listen to music, eat, ice-skate and discover, as well as simply to enjoy a garden. The site continues to grow, innovate and conserve. A recent initiative is the planting of a forest of *Sequoia sempervirens* (Californian redwoods), a species endangered in the wild. In March 2016, forty saplings (basal shoots and clones of cuttings from living redwoods) were planted along the entrance road to Eden. It's estimated that by 2050 they should reach twenty-five metres in height, and in time could make over 100 metres.

Sir Tim has always been clear. 'Eden isn't a botanical garden. It isn't a collection of plants. It's a form of educational theatre designed to instill in visitors the importance of plants and of wonder at what they do and are.' He adds, 'Eden… is a powerful symbol of connection: between us and Nature, and of us to each other, where through the metaphor of plants we can see that what we share is far greater than what divides us.'

Above: The Titan arum flower opens for only forty-eight hours, and smells of rotting flesh.

Facing page: The Core building, based on the structure of a sunflower, houses interactive exhibits including a giant nutcracker.

Lamorran House Gardens

Above: Robert and Maria Antonietta Dudley-Cooke.

Facing page: Looking out to sea past St Anthony's Lighthouse.

Lamorran House Gardens lie on a steeply sloping four-acre (1.6 ha) site within the town of St Mawes, with spectacular views across Falmouth bay and out to sea past St Anthony's Lighthouse. Begun in 1982, the gardens contain one of the most extraordinary contemporary collections of plants in Cornwall.

Robert Dudley-Cooke is a passionate gardener. He remembers, at the age of nineteen, designing and building a garden in his first house in the southeast of England. 'It was a tiny courtyard,' he recalls, 'but I knew exactly the sort of Japanese garden I wanted to make within it. My parents were keen gardeners but their borders of short-lived riotous colour held no interest for me.' He also remembers his grandmother's garden quite clearly, and it was here that his interest in Japanese gardening began. 'The garden was within a large parkland setting, with extensive planting and formal flowerbeds, but what I recall quite clearly was the simple line of a Japanese pond with foliage mirroring its edge.'

An interest in rhododendrons and azaleas came along with his interest in the design elements of Japanese gardening, and Robert became a member of the Royal Horticultural Society's Rhododendron Committee, eventually creating a Japanese-style garden

within the five-acre (2 ha) grounds of a large Queen Anne house. He not only used Japanese plants and trees, but its design – complete with stones and raked gravel – was his interpretation of the traditional principles and concepts of this style of gardening.

Always keen to see new gardens, and to add to his ever-growing collection of rhododendrons and camellias, Robert and his Italian wife Maria Antonietta first visited Cornwall in the late 1970s. 'We were astonished by what we saw,' he says. 'Here were my favourite Japanese varieties, but growing virtually frost-free in woodland settings alongside a whole new range of sub-tropical species.' As visits to Cornwall became more frequent, car loads of plants were taken home to Surrey.

Within a few years those same plants were travelling in the opposite direction, when in 1982 the Dudley-Cookes decided to move to Cornwall. Now, though, three articulated lorries were needed to transport the thousands of specimens – particularly azaleas – that Robert had collected. The couple had considered purchasing Trebah, but saw the potential of the land surrounding Lamorran House to create a new garden to their specific vision.

Top: There are over 200 palms at Lamorran.

Above: Satsuki late-flowering bi-colour azaleas.

Tree ferns around the Roman Waterfall. From left: Cyathea dealbata, Dicksonia squarrosa, Cyathea cunninghamii *and* Dicksonia squarrosa.

'When we arrived there was virtually no garden as such,' says Robert. 'There was some amount of herbaceous planting and a copse, but generally the land was not cultivated and it was smothered in blackthorn and bramble.' For months Robert and Maria Antonietta lived and worked in London from Monday to Friday, spending their weekends in St Mawes clearing the site. 'The work to clear the undergrowth was in three stages,' Robert remembers. 'I began, on a ladder, cutting branches with loppers and secateurs. The second stage was to chainsaw the trunks of the self-seeded trees and brambles, and then the third was to physically dig out the roots.'

The design of the garden was based on three principles, which hold true today. First, Robert decided there should be no straight

Above: Butia yatay.

Facing page: Trachycarpus fortunei *and* Agave americana *opposite* Chamaerops humilis *and the Venetian bridge.*

lines; second, there should be as many changes of level as possible, and third, there should be water. Now, on a south-facing site in maritime Cornwall, with the chance of growing exotic and sub-tropical plants, and inspired by frequent visits to Mediterranean gardens in Italy and the south of France, a whole new catalogue of planting possibilities opened up. Yuccas, acacia, echeveria, agaves and aloes were about to be grown in St Mawes.

Palms were to play an important part in the gardens, and today there are over 200 specimens of some forty different varieties. It's thought that Lamorran is the most northerly palm garden in the world. There are several large specimens of *Butia capitata* (as well as examples of *B. yatay*, *B. odorata* and *B. eriospatha*). Some *Phoenix caneriensis* are almost eight metres high, and *P. roebelenii*, *P. theoprasti* and *P. reclinata* add interest alongside other varieties of *Brahea*, *Washingtonia* and *Parajubea*. The one palm Robert recommends for hardiness, however, is *Chamerops humilis*. 'It more than matches the *Trachycarpus* species for strength and vigour.'

'In the early days it was quite hard to source palms and tree ferns,' says Robert. 'Many had to come direct from Italy, but they've all done incredibly well.' Now there are extensive plantings of tree ferns, including *Dicksonia squarrosa* (as well as the more familiar *Dicksonia antarctica*). The *Cyathea* tree ferns are popular too, with the black-stemmed *C. medullaris* a particular favourite. New plantings of *C. australis* and *C. cooperi* are made as plant material becomes available.

Many of the focal points have vistas out over the sea.

Robert's early love of Japanese rhododendrons and azaleas is still evident, however. 'I must have propagated over one thousand azaleas in Surrey and they have all found a home here. The evergreen varieties are particularly special to me, we get six months flowering from them and the bicolours are especially striking.'

The hard landscaping is a particular feature at Lamorran. Robert superimposed the careful placing of bridges, steps, statuary, ruined walls, temples and gazebos over his original designs. Taking inspiration from Italian gardens such as La Mortola he has created a wealth of focal points within the garden, many of which lead to vistas out over the sea.

In addition to the sea's moderating effect, an early shelterbelt of *Griselina littoralis* (since reduced) as well as other judicious planting to filter the wind, has meant that Lamorran House Gardens now boasts an extraordinary micro-climate and is ranked a 'Zone 10' garden. Virtually frost-free from 1987, this means that Lamorran has similar conditions to parts of Miami, Southern California and stretches of the Mediterranean coast, which it resembles so closely.

Robert did all the garden work himself for many years, but in 1995 Mark Brent, a Kew student, came to work alongside him. Ned Lomax left the National Trust's Glendurgan garden to become Head Gardener at Lamorran in 2015, and he is now heavily involved in further developing the lower part of the garden, as well as with a variety of new projects.

Robert and Maria Antonietta have recently developed a formal Edwardian-style structured rose garden near the house. It's walled on two sides with pillars, linking chains, trellis and a summerhouse. Planted with over 250 old fashioned scented roses, in shades of white through to mid-pink, it offers a total contrast to the rest of the garden.

After the early work had been done, in 1990 Robert and Maria Antonietta responded to requests from local people to open their garden to the public on occasional days. The open days were so successful that Lamorran House Gardens has opened regularly since 1992, and is currently open from April to September each year.

Top: The formal rose garden near the house is in the Edwardian style.

Above: Ned Lomax (left) and Robert Dudley-Cooke.

16 February 1990 is a date that will live for ever in Cornish garden history. It was on that day that Tim Smit and John Willis began the project that *The Times* would call 'the garden restoration of the century', when they macheted and chopped their way through tangled briars and giant rhododendrons and discovered the site of what was once a magnificent Edwardian garden.

The Lost Gardens of Heligan occupies some 200 acres (80 ha), partly within a valley setting, leading down to the sea at Mevagissey on the south coast of Cornwall. The name 'Heligan' first appeared in 1203, but it was exactly 400 years later that William Tremayne built his new home here. Over the generations the house was extended, and eventually rebuilt in 1803 by Henry Hawkins Tremayne. It remains privately owned to this day.

Following his elder brother's death, Henry seized the opportunities offered by his unexpected inheritance. In 1774, he commissioned a survey of the entire estate from William Hole; the exquisitely drawn map can still be seen in the Cornwall Record Office. He went on to order 'Proposals for Development' from one Thomas Gray, and started work. Shelterbelts were planted, field boundaries removed, rides laid out, shrubberies planted, and the Melon Yard, Northern Summerhouse

The Lost Gardens of Heligan

Top: Tim Smit (left) and John Nelson – the early days.

Above: Henry Hawkins Tremayne.

Facing page: The Melon Yard.

and Flower Garden built. As early as 1824, Heligan was attracting attention:

> 'The gardens… are cultivated with much care, and the hot-houses furnish a great variety of curious and aromatic plants.' (Fortescue Hitchins, The History of Cornwall, Helston, 1824)

Henry's son, John Hearle Tremayne, continued his father's investment in the Heligan estate. He married Caroline Lemon from Carclew, whose family sponsored the expeditions of plant hunter Joseph Hooker, among others. Perhaps more than any other Victorian explorer, Hooker was responsible for rhododendron mania in Britain. After four years in Sikkim – a tiny Himalayan kingdom – he brought back forty-three new species, many of which found homes at Heligan.

Top: The Flower Garden.

Above: John Hearle Tremayne.

John Tremayne became Squire in 1851 and, with his wife the Honorable Mary Vivian, developed the planting at Heligan, such that by the 1890s it was achieving national recognition. Hybridization was the new craze, with *Rhododendron* 'Cornish Red', *R.* 'John Tremayne', and *R.* 'Heljackii' flowering in the gardens. The lawns and flower gardens were places of recreation, with a monkey, a parrot and even emus adding to the feeling of exoticism:

> *'Mrs Tremayne's garden more nearly approaches my own ideal of what an old English flower garden ought to be like more than anything I have ever seen.'* (The Gardeners' Chronicle, *19 December 1896)*

It was during the ownership of John Claude (Jack) Tremayne that the gardens at Heligan would undergo dramatic and irrevocable change. The outbreak of the First World War meant that the number of outdoor staff on the estate was cut from twenty-three to eight. A poignant reminder of the time was the discovery of the signatures of some of the garden staff on the flaking lime plaster on the wall of the 'thunderbox' (the gardeners' lavatory). Thirteen Heligan men enlisted; nine gave their lives. Today, the site is registered by the Imperial War Museum as a 'Living Memorial'.

Jack offered Heligan House as a convalescent hospital for officers of the Royal Flying Corps, and moved to Italy in 1923. Over the years it was tenanted and then used as a billet for American army troops during rehearsals at nearby Pentewan for the D-Day landings in 1944. In 1973 it was converted into flats and then sold off. Over a quarter of a century, nature was left to reclaim the gardens.

With his then wife Candy, Tim Smit had moved to Cornwall in 1987 and was living in a nearby farmhouse. The director of Newquay Zoo, Rob Poole, had lent them two Vietnamese potbellied pigs to clear their land. A plan to keep other rare breeds as a tourist attraction meant that larger premises were needed, and a chance meeting with John Willis, a member of the Tremayne family, led to the day on which Tim and John set out to discover whether the Heligan estate might be suitable.

Top: John Tremayne.

Above: John Claude Tremayne.

It was when they saw an old vine, clinging to life among the shards of glass and rotten timbers from the greenhouse that once sheltered it, that the idea of restoring the gardens took hold. Tim's builder, John Nelson, began clearance and Philip McMillan Browse, the Cornwall County Council Horticultural Adviser, was brought in to advise on the plant treasures that were being discovered on a daily basis.

The relationship between the garden and its visitors has always been very special at Heligan. Candy Smit, who is still involved with the garden, explains:

'This is a working garden and our visitors see work being done every day, all year round. They share our successes and our failures and have easy access to staff – for information or even just for a chat. The gardens are managed in a traditionally labour-intensive fashion, using many of the old ways. This triggers fond memories in older visitors and new interests for younger ones. Education and conservation run hand-in-hand alongside fresh food on the table.'

Top: The original lean-to vinery in the Flower Garden.

Above: The gardens are worked using the old ways.

Iain Davies is the current Head of Gardens and Estate, and is keen to show visitors as many gardening techniques as possible, even within period-correct areas such as the Productive Gardens, while cherishing the plant heritage that the gardens hold. Heligan was the first garden in Britain to propagate *Cornus capitata* (originally known as *Benthamia fragifera*), and it became the centrepiece of its earliest horticultural reputation, after the then Head Gardener, J. Roberts, succeeded in germinating seed sent from Nepal. In 1832 a new

drive to Heligan House was created, and a large number of these seedling trees were planted along its length. The resulting sight was so impressive that it was reported in several national magazines, but by 1990 only one tree remained. Once the ground beneath it had been cleared, it self-seeded, and the drive has become lined with *Cornus capitata* once again.

Another of Heligan's success stories is *Rhododendron niveum*. Heligan's original specimens would have been planted during the 1850s as part of the great rhododendron boom. However, by the 1870s the variety had spectacularly fallen from favour for the simple reason that its flower's particular shade of purple was virtually the same as a new chemical dye, mauveine, which was used for the mass-produced uniforms of hospital nurses and domestic staff. Through sheer snobbery, head gardeners across the country were instructed to root out the plants. At Heligan, one specimen survived and can still be seen at the back of Flora's Green.

Top: Ian Davies.

Above: Rhododendron niveum.

Despite the richness and variety of The Lost Gardens of Heligan's historic plant stock, the garden is perhaps best known to the public for its pineapples (*Ananas comosus*). The extraordinarily labour-intensive way they were (and are) grown has attracted interest from around the world, and for many visitors, spending time examining the brick pigeonholing and the pits in which the pineapples grow under glass, heated by rotting horse manure from local stables, is the highlight of their visit. The traditional varieties 'Jamaica Queen' and 'Smooth Cayenne' are popular, and one of Heligan's first fruits was presented to Her Majesty the Queen at the time of her Golden Wedding Anniversary.

A founding member of The Great Gardens of Cornwall, Heligan was one of the first gardens in the county to stay open all year round to provide employment and to sustain the restoration project long-term. Since opening in 1992, the gardens have won dozens of major awards, for tourism, heritage, horticulture and environment. They have helped to pioneer new micro-propagation techniques, hosted seasonal events, and welcomed well over five million visitors.

Top and facing page:
Fruit ripens in the pineapple pit.

Above: A barn owl in the grounds.

The National Trust

Above and facing page:
Antony, with its fine yew hedges.

The National Trust is a special member of The Great Gardens of Cornwall, jointly representing its seven Cornish garden properties: Antony, near Torpoint; Cotehele, on the banks of the Tamar; Glendurgan, on the Helford river; Godolphin, near Helston; Lanhydrock, near Bodmin; Trelissick, near Truro, and Trengwainton, in west Cornwall.

Antony

The Carew family has lived at Antony, overlooking the River Lynher, since the late-fifteenth century. Richard Carew built a 'fishful pond' on the shores of the river, with a palisade to keep out scavenging otters, and a floodgate to let sea water in, but virtually nothing is known of the garden at this time. The present house dates from 1711, when it was built in the Georgian style by Richard's great-great-grandson, Sir William. Drawings from some fifteen years later show tree-lined avenues and formal beds on the estate, but it was after suggestions from Humphry Repton, who wrote one of his famous Red Books about Antony for then-owner Reginald Pole Carew, that significant changes began to be made.

Views to the river were opened up (framed by *Quercus ilex* – holm oak), yew hedges planted, and kitchen gardens established. There is an historic knot garden, and in the early twentieth

century, fine collections of rhododendrons, camellias and magnolias were established. Antony is host to the National Collection of Hemerocallis (daylilies), which includes over 600 cultivars bearing names such as 'Sir John' and 'Antony House'.

Cotehele House

Carew's 1602 *Survey of Cornwall* describes Cotehele's buildings as 'large strong and fair and appurtananced with the necessities of wood, water, fishing, parks and mills'. Owned for many years by the Edgcumbe family, the gardens were not formally laid out until the mid-nineteenth century.

As part of renovations to the house in 1862, three terraces were created to its eastern side. Nowadays, these are formally planted with a range of herbaceous plants with a pastel theme. The Valley Garden has a wildflower meadow and is the site of a thatched Victorian summerhouse and a medieval stew-pond. In the Upper Garden, two deep borders show contrasting planting – the north side in shades of red, orange and yellow, and the west in gold and silver, following a plan by Gardens Adviser Graham Stuart Thomas.

The Tamar valley has a rich tradition of fruit growing, and Cotehele boasts two orchards: the 'Mother' orchard, planted in 2007, cultivates and curates some 120 local, traditional apple varieties; the other is older – it is shown on a 1731 map of the estate – and grows Tamar cherries, pears and walnuts, as well as apples.

Cotehele. The eastern terraces (top). The dovecote (above).

Glendurgan Garden

Like its neighbour, Trebah Garden, Glendurgan owes its early development to members of the famous Fox family. Quakers, and

both merchants and bankers, they were keen gardeners, and also established notable estates in and around Falmouth at Penjerrick, Rosehill and Greatwood. Glendurgan, with its house at the head of a valley running down to the Helford estuary, was planted by Alfred Fox in the early 1800s. He introduced both the first version of the iconic maze and the tulip trees on the east side of the valley.

Since the National Trust took over the garden in 1962, the development of the garden has continued. Four *Trachycarpus fortunei* (Chusan palms) now mark the corners of the maze of *Prunus laurocerasus* (cherry laurel), and a thatched summerhouse sits at its centre. Elsewhere, tree ferns and succulents have been planted, along with epiphytic plants that grow easily on trunks and branches in Cornwall's moist, warm climate.

Glendurgan. Tulip trees and Chusan palms flourish in the valley (top). The iconic maze of cherry laurel (above).

Godolphin. The house (top). Seasonal planting in the side garden (above).

Godolphin Estate

Godolphin House is a relatively recent acquisition for the National Trust, but it is one of Cornwall's most ancient homes. The Godolphin family was rich and powerful, with a fortune built on tin during the sixteenth and seventeenth centuries. Their wealth was shown by the creation of a deer park and a rabbit warren, and by developing their estate with substantial planting and avenues of trees.

An estate map of 1786 shows side and pond gardens set out as nine hedged plots with dividing walkways. It's thought that these fashionable designs were inspired by those drawn up by John Gerard for the estate of Lord Burghley in Hertfordshire, as both feature nine compartments linked in a similar way. The garden at Godolphin also held a semi-ornamental orchard and a pond for breeding fish.

Since acquiring Godolphin Estate in 2007, the National Trust has carried out extensive work to both the house and the garden. In the house, the King's Room is now an exhibition space; outdoors, the King's Garden has pruned box hedges and large magnolias. The side garden also has traditional, seasonal planting in three of the original nine Tudor compartments.

Lanhydrock House

The first Lanhydrock House was built of Cornish granite on an ecclesiastical foundation amid acres of surrounding parkland. Today, it's a wonderful example of high Victorian style, as are the formal gardens, following well-known garden designer George Truefitt's plans of 1854. At the front of the house is an ornate gatehouse, which separates the parkland from the garden. Formal flowerbeds with mature specimen yews (*Taxus baccata*) add a

Lanhydrock. The formal gardens (top). The ornate gatehouse and specimen yews (above).

Trelissick. The Water Tower and orchard (top). Gardeners Guss Lilly and John Reid, 1900.

further degree of symmetry to the main approach to the house.

For many gardeners, the higher ground to the rear of the house provides the most interest, for it is here that the estate's collection of towering magnolias and camellias grows. *Magnolia grandiflora* flourishes against the wall of the house itself, but on the raised terraces above are over 100 different species, including *M. campbellii* ssp. *mollicomata* 'Peter Borlase' (named after a former head gardener). Mature rhododendrons also grow here, with other spring- and summer-flowering shrubs, including hydrangeas and azaleas.

Trelissick Garden

Trelissick House was built in the mid-eighteenth century by John Lawrence, a Captain in the Cornwall militia. In 1800, the estate was bought by the wealthy Daniell family (mine-owner Thomas Daniell was known as 'Guinea-a-Minute Daniell' because of the money he'd made during the Cornish tin boom). They added the famous porticos to the façade, and developed the estate, creating miles of rides through the woods bordering the creeks leading off the River Fal.

The present garden owes much to the planting done by the last owners of the house. The garden had been mainly shrubbery, with some good trees and conifers, but Ronald and Ida Copeland (who inherited Trelissick in 1937) added rhododendrons, camellias, azaleas and hydrangeas, taking advantage of the mild maritime climate.

The National Trust has developed the garden extensively since then. A walled sensory garden, just inside the entrance, adds texture and scent before a huge wisteria leads to a series of borders planted with palms, bananas and dahlias. A thatched summerhouse overlooking the water carries the names of some of the head gardeners who have contributed to the popularity of the garden.

Trengwainton Garden

A carved granite stone near Trengwainton House proclaims that the estate was acquired by the powerful Arundell family in 1692. In 1814, the house was bought by Sir Rose Price, who owned a sugar plantation in Jamaica. He set about a programme of improvements that included building a series of walled gardens (bizarrely, to the dimensions of Noah's ark), and creating sloping, raised beds for growing vegetables. He died within a year of the 1833 Emancipation Act, and the family had to sell the estate.

In 1867, the well-known Cornish Bolitho family became the garden's owners, and they improved it out of all recognition. In 1926, Lieutenant-Colonel Edward Bolitho bought a share in planthunter Frank Kingdon Ward's expedition to Assam and Burma. Seeds and young plants became the core of an impressive collection of rhododendrons, including *Rhododendron macabeanum*, *R. elliottii* and *R. concatenans*.

Now the kitchen garden is grown using organic principles, and the orchard contains a restored Victorian bee-house with a live colony, as well as a magnificent maidenhair tree (*Ginkgo biloba*). A stream, planted with primulas and iris, runs alongside the drive, and the distant views over Mount's Bay are impressive.

Trengwainton. Rhododendrons and azaleas (top). Primulas by the stream (above).

Trebah Garden

Above: Charles Fox bought the estate at Trebah in 1838 and created a garden in the valley.

Facing page: Originally planted for the cut-flower market in the 1950s, there are still two acres (0.8 ha) of blue hydrangeas in the lower part of the valley.

Trebah Garden is set on the banks of the famous Helford river in south Cornwall, in a sheltered, wooded valley that leads down to a private beach. Originally planted nearly 200 years ago, it boasts 5,000 plants from around the world, and four miles of footpaths.

The estate at Trebah dates back to the Domesday Survey of 1085–6, when the land was owned by the Bishop of Exeter. It then passed from generation to generation through many historic Cornish families, but its real development began in 1838 when it was bought by Charles Fox. A member of the well-known local Quaker family, shipping agent and Manager of Perran Foundry, he set about creating a garden in the south-facing valley. Like others in his family, he was a keen horticulturist and had access to some of the new plants and seeds then being brought to England from overseas.

Charles Fox recognized the importance of creating shelter for the specimens he was importing, and planted hundreds of *Pinus radiata* (Monterey pines) and *Quercus ilex* (Holm oak) to create shelterbelts either side of the valley. A second line of shelter was created lower down the slopes with beech trees (*Fagus sylvatica* and *F. sylvatica* 'Purpurea'). Charles's brother Robert was a great friend of plant hunter

Joseph Hooker – who later (1865–85) became Director of Kew Gardens. Hooker was a prolific collector of rhododendrons, and it is thought that Trebah's early stock came from his travels in Tibet, Nepal and Bhutan.

Charles was passionate about the garden and, to make sure he was siting his new plants in exactly the correct location to preserve the view, had a scaffold tower built to represent their ultimate height. A garden boy with a flag sat atop this structure as it was manhandled from place to place, while Charles, looking through a telescope from the house, shouted instructions through a megaphone.

He bequeathed the estate to his daughter, Juliet, and her husband Edmund Backhouse, who continued to maintain the garden with Head Gardener Harry Thomas and a team of fifteen gardeners. In 1880, a shipment of 3,000 tree-fern trunks (*Dicksonia antarctica*) arrived at Falmouth docks as ballast on a ship from New Zealand. Of these, 300 were planted at Trebah, expanding the plant collection even further.

In 1907 Trebah was purchased by Charles Hext, High Sheriff of Cornwall, and his wife Alice. Aided by a large team of gardeners, they too added to the diversity of the plant collection. Ponds were created and stocked with

Above: Alice Hext came to Trebah in 1907.

Facing page: In the mid-nineteenth century, the garden benefited from Joseph Hooker's expeditions to Tibet, Nepal and Bhutan. Rhododendrons were a particular enthusiasm.

A natural spring feeds ponds in the valley. Primulas and bugle (top) and Gunnera manicata *(giant rhubarb) thrive here.*

fish and flamingoes, and the garden became the location for many fashionable social gatherings.

In 1935, at the invitation of Alice Hext, the then Prince of Wales (later and briefly Edward VIII) brought a party to the garden, including both Wallis and Ernest Simpson. Perhaps apocryphal, a story is still told that the Prince was much impressed by a clump of banana plants, laden with perfect, ripe fruit, growing near the house. He congratulated the Head Gardener, Mr Day, and gave him a sovereign for his efforts. The next day Mr Day was reprimanded – not for tying the bought fruit to the plants to impress the guests, but for leaving one of the 'Elders & Fyffes' labels still in place!

Alice Hext died in 1939, and the Second World War brought huge change to Trebah. The estate was split up, and the farm sold separately. In 1944, access roads for military vehicles were built, leading around the coast path. The beach at the bottom of the garden was covered in concrete, and a jetty built out into the Helford, despite Messerschmitt attacks. On 1 June, some 7,500 soldiers from the US 29th Infantry Division marched along the newly constructed roads to the beach from where they embarked in ten flat-bottomed landing craft laden with tanks and guns for the D-Day landings at Omaha beach in Normandy. Very few would survive.

Over the next twenty years, Trebah changed hands five times until, in 1961, it was bought by Donald Healey, the racing driver and car designer. He used the house's outbuildings to construct prototypes of Rolls Royce engines and chassis for Jensen-Healey, and built a boathouse on the beach as a base for the air/sea rescue inflatables he designed for the Ministry of Defence.

In 1981 Trebah was bought by Major Tony Hibbert and his wife Eira as a retirement home. 'We dreamt of the quiet pleasures of retirement, mornings spent drinking gin on the terrace and summer afternoons fishing and sailing from the beach,' he said. But the dream was not to come true. The Hibberts began to realize the heritage of the garden they had bought, and sought expert advice. They were persuaded to begin a programme of restoration by the Cornwall Garden Society, and opened to the public in 1987 to help cover the cost of the work. Three years later they donated the house and garden to the Trebah Garden Trust, a registered charity. The garden is still run by a board of trustees.

Major Hibbert's extraordinary wartime story (a member of the Parachute Brigade who held the bridge at Arnhem against overwhelming odds, and was then captured but escaped) is reflected in the garden. Ninky's Pool and Dinky's Puddle are named after Hiltje and Nienke Van Eck, two girls whose parents sheltered Tony Hibbert and his comrades after Arnhem. Memorials to the men of the Parachute Regiment, and to the US 29th Infantry Division, stand near the beach, and an annual Military Day is held. The Major also told the story of Heino Braumüller, a German visitor to the garden in the 1980s, who told Tony that he had flown over Trebah

Top: The beach below the garden from which, in 1944, soldiers embarked for the D-Day landings at Omaha beach.

Above: Tony Hibbert bought Trebah in 1981, and later donated the house and garden to the Trebah Garden Trust.

in May 1944 in a Junkers 88 on a mission to destroy shipping in Falmouth harbour, and his plane had been fired on by the anti-aircraft guns on the beach. For forty years, he had remembered quite clearly what he thought was a beautiful house and garden, and the two men were to become firm friends.

Darren Dickey has been Head Gardener at Trebah since 2002, though he has been at the garden for much longer and has been involved in horticulture all his life. 'I remember many days after school and at weekends gardening with my granddad,' he says. 'I loved working in his garden or in the greenhouse.' Darren studied horticulture at Duchy College Rosewarne and, through the course, worked at neighbouring Glendurgan garden.

Part of his responsibility is the two acres (0.8 ha) of blue hydrangeas in the lower part of the valley. These were originally planted in the 1950s for the cut-flower market, and sent to Covent Garden on the overnight Cornish flower train to London. That no longer happens, but each year hundreds of flower-heads are sent to Derbyshire, for use in traditional well-dressing ceremonies.

Top: Davidia involucrata (*the handkerchief tree*) *in the Chilean Coomb.*

Above: Head Gardener Darren Dickey admires Magnolia campbellii.

A favourite part of the garden for Darren is the Chilean Coomb. 'As well as the general planting there are three very special trees there,' he says. 'First of all there's a huge *Davidia involucrata* var. *vilmoriniana* (handkerchief tree), then a magnificent *Magnolia campbellii* and a *Laureliopsis philippiana* (a rare evergreen tree from Chile and Argentina).'

Phyllostachys edulis
*(the giant timber bamboo),
which can grow more than
20 cm every day.*

Trebah is also famous for its 'Bamboozle' – an internationally important collection of bamboos. 'We have rarer varieties,' says Darren, 'but the one visitors always want to see is *Phyllostachys edulis* (the giant timber bamboo), which can grow at a rate of more than 20 cm every day and has canes up to 30 cm in circumference. People come back each day just to photograph its growth. I love working in the garden and it's always great to receive positive feedback from our visitors, both in person and on social media.'

Trebah Garden is open every day of the year.

The home of the Boscawen family, Tregothnan lies close to Cornwall's south coast, and is one of the largest private gardens in the country. As well as holding a wonderful plant collection, the estate pioneered the growing of British tea and is the only producer of Manuka honey outside New Zealand.

Tregothnan means 'the house at the head of the valley', and it was here that John de Boscawen came when he married Joan de Tregothnan in 1334. Remarkably, the house has been kept within the family ever since. The only remaining visible element of the original Tudor house is a simple doorway at the entrance to the kitchen garden, for in the 1650s the house was rebuilt by Hugh Boscawen. It was described by Celia Fiennes, a late seventeenth-century visitor, as

*'of white stone… the entrance is up
a few steps into a large high hall.
On the left hand is a great parlour
and drawing roome wainscoted all
very well, but plaine'.*

Hugh Boscawen's nephew inherited, and was created Viscount Falmouth for services to George I. In 1811, Humphry Repton, the architect and landscape designer, was commissioned to survey the house, as he was other Cornish mansions, but at Tregothnan his report also contained plans for land-

*Above: The Tudor doorway
at the entrance to the kitchen
garden.*

Facing page: Camellia maze.

scaping the grounds. Later, the fourth Viscount was created the first Earl of Falmouth at George IV's coronation, and subsequently employed William Wilkins, architect of the National Gallery in Trafalgar Square, to enlarge and redesign the house in the 1820s.

There was little garden to speak of when Celia Fiennes came to Tregothnan. She recorded 'gravel walks round and across' and 'an orchard which is something like a grove,' but added, 'it is capable of being a fine place with some change.' It was the sixth Viscount Falmouth, Evelyn Boscawen, who, in the mid-nineteenth century, brought about that change, much of which is retained in the layout of the present gardens, which cover some 100 acres (40 ha) within the overall estate. It was he, along with his brother John Townsend Boscawen, who planted several varieties of the newly fashionable *Camellia japonica*.

Camellias thrived at Tregothnan, and they are an important part of the garden today. The present owner, the Honourable Evelyn Boscawen, says that *Camellia reticulata* 'Captain Rawes' is one of his favourite plants. It was named after the Captain of the clipper *Warren Hastings*, who had brought the plant from China in 1820. 'Our first plant, long since gone, had astonishing dimensions,' he says, 'but we've managed to cultivate a few sizeable specimens from our original.'

A new collection of *Camellia sasanqua* lines the Farm Drive. Many of them were brought here from a monk's collection in Kyoto. They start to flower in November and have a delicate scent and butterfly-like, fragile-looking flowers. Descendants of the early plantings of *Camellia japonica* – 'Canon Boscawen', 'Hornsby Pink' and others – are still in the garden and, in the lower area, are several hundred *Camellia sinensis*.

The commercial growing of *Camellia sinensis* has been one of Tregothnan's biggest success stories in recent years. The topography of the estate and the proximity of the River Fal give the garden its own microclimate. It was thought that if camellias grew well generally, then surely the tea plant – itself a camellia – would also flourish. Early plantings were successful, and the first

Top: Garden Director Jonathon Jones in the tea plantation.

Above: The Honourable Evelyn Boscawen (left) with the High Commissioner for India at Tregothnan.

Facing page: The 'Himalayan Valley' tea plantation.

Above: Sir Joseph Hooker.

Facing page: Rhododendron arboreum *'Cornish Red' arch over a drive.*

commercial crop was harvested in 2005. The new growth is plucked from the thousands of shoots by hand, then dried and processed to be marketed by the estate. Since 2005, various varieties have been developed, and Tregothnan tea has become an iconic British brand.

Another relatively recent development has been the construction of a new parterre at the front of the house. Replacing a design of 1845, landscape architect Robert Myers has made a striking grass parterre for the present owner. It includes two reflection pools within gravelled paths; these have the effect of enhancing the view by leading the eye toward the river.

Tregothnan is home to one of Cornwall's greatest collections of rhododendrons. Like others of the Great Gardens, the estate benefitted from the expeditions of Sir Joseph Hooker, with plantings of *Rhododendron sinogrande*, and *R. falconeri* in particular. Mr Boscawen remembers, 'It was rhododendrons which gave me my first interest in the garden when I entered a competitive class at the Cornwall Flower Show to display different rhododendron leaves. I remember my entry ranged from *Rhododendron sinogrande* (the largest) to *R.* 'Blue Tit' (the smallest).'

Rhododendron arboreum 'Cornish Red' plays a special part in the garden. It is planted around much of the Summer

House Lawns, and provides a mass of crimson flowers in April and May. Other varieties here include *R. ciliatum* and *R.* 'Loderi King George', though *R. griffithianum* (formerly *R. aucklandii*), whose flowers bud pink but bloom white is a favourite. There is also a new collection of species rhododendrons in the more sheltered and damp Himalayan Valley.

Close to this part of the garden is a collection of South American plants put together by Garden Director Jonathon Jones. He has travelled extensively in this region on three occasions, visiting Chile, Brazil, Argentina, Ecuador and Colombia, in part following the route taken by Cornish Victorian plant hunter William Lobb. As children, William and his brother Thomas lived on the Pencarrow Estate near Bodmin, but moved to Perranarworthal near Truro, working for the famous Veitch nurseries. William found forests of *Araucaria araucana* in Chile and brought home saplings, nicknamed 'monkey puzzle' trees by a visitor to Pencarrow. Normally seen as single specimens, a glade of them has been established at Tregothnan.

'To retrace William's steps was an unforgettable experience,' says Jonathon. 'The conditions in which he travelled and worked must have been very hard, but I can imagine the thrill he must have felt to discover new plants growing in the same conditions he'd left behind in Cornwall.'

One of the plants introduced by Jonathon to Tregothnan is so rare that, as yet, it is unnamed. A climbing hydrangea, it is evergreen with dark green, glossy leaves. It was found growing in conditions similar to those in the garden and, so far, is thriving.

Another of the garden's newer star plants is *Wollemia nobilis* (the Wollemi pine), which is also a member of Araucariaceae. For years, this multiple-trunked conifer was known only in fossilized form, and was believed to be extinct. Then, in Australia in 1994, a bush walker named David Noble came across a living specimen growing in a deep ravine within a National Park, only 100 miles from Sydney. His discovery took the horticultural world by storm, and the tree has become as popular with twenty-first century gardeners as did the introductions of the Victorian plant hunters in their day.

The past and present are inextricably linked for the Honourable Evelyn Boscawen and the Tregothnan team. Mr Boscawen and his wife Katharine say they are particularly inspired by the *Magnolia campbellii*, planted by his grandfather in 1923. It flowers for a month from mid-February, and they regard it as a sign of spring and the beginning of their gardening year. It also stands as a reminder of the ongoing development of the garden through the generations, and is a symbol of its richness and strength.

Tregothnan is open for pre-booked private parties all year round, and to the general public on special charity weekends.

Top: Wollemia nobilis *(Wollemi pine) – the first male and female cones borne outside Australia.*

Above: Araucaria araucana *(monkey puzzle).*

Facing page: Rhododendron *'Loderi King George'.*

Tregrehan

Home to the Carlyon family since the sixteenth century, Tregrehan lies just outside St Austell, about a mile from the coast. An owner's passion for trees in the nineteenth century ensured that the collection of camellias for which the garden also became famous, was sheltered and they thrived in the mild Cornish climate.

The early gardens at Tregrehan were close to the house, with a deer park to the south when the Edgcumbe and Bodrugan families originally owned the estate, but it passed to the Carlyons in 1565 and Tregrehan House itself was built by Thomas Carlyon and his son. A wealthy mine owner, Philip Carlyon, inherited in 1734. He also had horticultural interests, selling trees such as laurels, elms and oaks, and planting up the area around the china clay stream known as 'Whitewater' with larch, laurel, fir, walnut and beech. Philip's son died childless, leaving the estate to his nephew, Thomas.

Other wealthy Cornish landowners had employed the great landscape designer Humphry Repton to design their gardens and parkland, and Carlyon, keen to be among their number, used a similar style – but not the man himself – to develop Tregrehan. Barns and a dairy complex were constructed, and Thomas's son, William, took over the building of a stable block

The yew walk, probably designed by Edward Carlyon with his garden architect, William Nesfield.

The nineteeth-century yew walk (top) and glasshouses (above).

and may have started planting the conifers for which the house became famous. He was also the recipient of some of the plants being brought back to the county by explorers overseas.

William died young in 1841, and was succeeded by his younger brother, Edward, who moved back to Tregrehan following a complete refurbishment of both the garden and the house, which had been redesigned in 1842 in a classical style by architect George Wightwick. Edward's interest lay primarily in the garden though, and with his garden architect William Nesfield, he designed the entrance court, the formal parterre, and probably the yew walk. Nesfield's original plan, dated 1843, is still preserved at the house. The walled garden had also been remodelled from two separate gardens, and impressively large glasshouses – nearly forty metres long – were erected.

Edward's own account books show that it was at this time that first-generation rhododendrons of those varieties found in Sikkim by Sir Joseph Hooker – knighted in 1877 for his horticultural discoveries – were planted in the garden. *Rhododendron grande*, *R. griffithianum*, and *R. falconeri* all date from this time. He also bought plants from the Veitch nurseries that had been collected by the Lobb brothers.

In the 1880s and 1890s, the garden continued to grow under the stewardship of Edward's grandson, Jovey Carlyon. An avid plant collector, during his time Tregrehan's plant stock soared, as the garden was supplied with plants by thirteen different nurseries, and by contacts all over the world. Gilbert Rogers, a Cornish forester living in Dehra Dun close to India's north-west frontier, sent him a letter dated 1 July 1894:

> 'I have sent you a box containing some seeds of Quercus semecarpifolia [brown oak] in charcoal… I hope some of them will reach you alive. This species… covers the highest hills in Yarmsa and so should do very well for you.'

An oak from that box of acorns now stands more than twenty-five metres tall.

By the time of the First World War, the gardens at Tregrehan were attracting attention. W.J. Bean, from the Royal Botanic Gardens, Kew wrote in detail about 'The Arboretum at Tregrehan', commenting especially on the collections of conifers and rhododendrons. Professor Sargent, of the Arnold Arboretum at Harvard University, called Tregrehan 'the best thing of its kind in the world.'

Top: Rhododendron falconeri – *a seedling from a Hooker plant.*

Above: Quercus semecarpifolia – *from an 1894 acorn.*

In 1935, Jovey's nephew, Rupert Carlyon, moved to Tregrehan from New Zealand, from where he imported a large amount of plant material. But the family had been absent from the property for some forty years, and between the wars only basic care and maintenance of the garden took place. However, Tregrehan took on a new lease of life in the 1960s when Rupert's daughter, Gillian, returned to the house and began a major camellia breeding programme. After clearing areas of the garden for her project, she set about propagating hybrids from the old plants on the estate. This resulted in a variety of new cultivars, including 'ETR Carlyon' (a white double) and 'Nijinsky' (a semi-double pink). She became famous for her specialized work, and was awarded the Reginald Cory Memorial Cup by the Royal Horticultural Society for her efforts in developing *Camellia* x *williamsii* 'Jenefer Carlyon' (a large, semi-double pink).

Tregrehan is now owned by Gillian's cousin, Tom Hudson, who is continuing the plant collecting work of his ancestors. Tom came to live at the house in 1987, and was first inspired by the stature and variety of the tree collection. 'The conifer collection at Tregrehan has always been especially interesting to me,' he says. 'From the Far East *Thuja standishii* [green giant] and *Thujopsis dolabrata* [Hiba cedar] are both exceptional and *Podocarpus totara* [tōtara tree], *P. hallii* [Hall's tōtara] and *P. salignus* [willow podocarp] from the Southern hemisphere are all large specimens now.' He adds, 'It's the size as well as the rarity of the trees that impresses our visitors; *Tsuga dumosa* [Himalayan hemlock] from the Himalaya and *Pseudotsuga menziesii* [Douglas fir] and *Cupres-*

Top: Camellia *x* williamsii *'Jenefer Carlyon' was developed by Gillian Carlyon (above, in later life).*

Facing page: Tom Hudson, present owner of Tregrehan, stands beneath Pseudotsuga menziesii *(Douglas fir).*

sus macrocarpa [Monterey cypress] from North America are all of monster size considering they're growing in the UK.'

As a result of the years of tree collecting, planting and cultivation, Tregrehan has well over 150 trees on the national Tree Register, which records the tallest and widest trees in the country. This is far more than any other single private garden in the UK. The overall feeling within the garden valley is of a temperate rainforest as it would have existed in Europe before the most recent ice age.

The International Conifer Conservation Programme set up by the Royal Botanic Garden Edinburgh has also brought many rare and endangered trees to Tregrehan. This project, which has been running for over twenty years, aims to grow seedlings of plants, under threat in their native habitat, within protected sites in the UK. Tregrehan was chosen to house many seedlings, especially from Chile and Taiwan, and they are now thriving in their new situation.

Tom Hudson has trialled a wide variety of Southern hemisphere plants in the garden. With his family links in New Zealand, useful contacts have enabled seed to be sourced and sent to Cornwall. It's then been grown on in the nursery before being planted in a dedicated two-acre (0.8 ha) section of the garden given over to native New Zealand species. He has also made a formal link with the Royal Botanic Gardens, Kew, which provides backup to this important and growing collection.

Tregrehan is open widely in the spring, less so in the summer.

Above: Thujopsis dolabrata *(Hiba cedar).*

Facing page: Cupressus macrocarpa *(Monterey cypress).*

Tremenheere Sculpture Gardens

Top: The granite bridge.

Above: The sheltering woods.

On a south-facing hillside overlooking the sweep of Mounts Bay and St Michael's Mount, Tremenheere Sculpture Gardens is unique among The Great Gardens of Cornwall. The site has no great history of gardening; there is no manor house at its centre; there is no emphasis on spring flowering, and contemporary art is at its heart.

Records reveal that prior to 1290 the land at Tremenheere was owned by the monks of the St Michael's Mount monastery. William de Tremenheere, probably a tenant farmer at that time, bought the land and started a line of ownership in which the owner carried the name of Tremenheere for some 600 years. The last family owner was Seymour Tremenheere, who died in 1894. He was a well-known national figure, a leading barrister and social reformer involved in improving conditions for mine workers and in schools. He also took a great interest in his estate, planting beech, oak, sweet chestnut and holly throughout the woods that shelter the land to the north and west, and creating a drive that wound its way up the slope to his summer retreat. A finely cut granite entrance bridge bears his initials and the date 1849.

Tremenheere found his land in good heart. It was said to be the site of a former vineyard, tended by the monks, and was a noted strawberry-growing

Top: One of several large ponds, fed by a stream.

Above: Neil Armstrong at Tremenheere.

and farming area (with produce being exported to Newfoundland). After his death, the Pearce family farmed the land for four generations. The acreage lies in a favoured spot, even by Cornish standards. Largely sheltered from the prevailing winds by woodland, and with a valley landscape, a stream runs through it and the site has several large ponds.

The present owners, Dr Neil Armstrong and his wife Dr Jane Martin, were also impressed by the natural qualities of the site when they first saw it in the 1990s. It lies within the so-called 'Golden Mile' – an area so blessed with good soil and virtually frost-free, sheltered conditions that tradition has it that farmers there can make extra income by harvesting more than one crop each season. pH levels range from 7.2 in what were the farmed areas to 4.6 in the woodland.

Neil Armstrong's mother was a garden designer and, doing various labouring jobs in the gardens on which she worked, he absorbed her classical approach, with a love of balance and symmetry.

Moving to Cornwall from Dublin in 1987, Neil and Jane were aware of Cornwall's garden heritage but lived here for some time before buying Tremenheere. 'I had no burning desire to build a big Cornish garden,' says Neil, 'but the opportunity just came along. It's always good to have a fresh challenge.'

While the site had great natural qualities (including wonderful views right across Mounts Bay from east to west), it had been severely neglected and, after buying it in 1997, Neil and Jane set about clearing scrub and woodland as well as still working full time as family doctors in Penzance (as they still do). Brambles and bracken dominated several acres; the ponds were virtually impenetrable swamp, and wild rhododendron was well established. The previously cropped land now grew luxuriant layers of weeds.

After just one year's work, a chance introduction was to change the development of the garden for ever. Both Neil and Jane are lovers of contemporary art, and a conversation with Emily Ash at Newlyn Art Gallery led to a meeting with renowned American artist James Turrell, the holder of many prestigious awards for both art and architecture. Trained in perceptual psychology and with a childhood fascination with light, much of his work is concerned with sky and space: 'I'm … interested in the sense of presence in space; that is space where you feel a presence, almost an entity – that physical feeling and power that space can give.'

Turrell was looking for a site from which he could interact with the solar eclipse of 1999. Cornwall was on the so-called 'line of

Tewlwolow Kernow –
James Turrell's Skyspace – an
underground elliptical domed
chamber from which to view the
sky, especially at twilight.

totality'; thousands of people were expected to come to the county to witness the spectacle, and authorities were on standby for official resources to be stretched to breaking point. With its sloping, open, south-facing aspect, Tremenheere was ideal. So began a liaison which continues to this day. *Tewlwolow Kernow* is permanently sited at a vantage point high in the garden. It's an elliptical, domed chamber, designed as a space from which to view the sky. On occasion, the Skyspace is internally lit with a soft white light that creates a magical interaction with the sky – both at dusk and at dawn. 'I found myself as unofficial project manager for the installation of Turrell's eclipse piece,' says Neil. 'It would have been a huge undertaking anywhere, but in a new garden like this where it was being sited on very rough ground where a potato crop had been taken out, the task was enormous.'

Above: Black Mound – *David Nash's charred oak shapes in mature woodland.*

Facing page: Cyathea medullaris *(black tree fern) is native to the south-west Pacific.*

Top: Forms, textures and colours harmonize with the landscape.
Above: Protea grandiceps *(Princess Protea) is native to South Africa.*

The installation, though, was to steer the garden development in a new direction. It spurred the concept of developing contemporary art in a garden landscape in a way which is new and exciting.

As planting continued over the years – the garden now boasts over forty varieties of palms, along with spectacular collections of grass trees, tree-ferns and bamboos – pieces of contemporary art and sculpture were sited at strategic locations. Some are permanent, some on loan, and many are the work of internationally respected artists and members of the Royal Academy.

Richard Long RA has created *Tremenheere Line* – a planted line of *Boloskion tetraphyllum* (South African restios) running due south from a point in the uppermost part of the garden. In the Quarry Space, Peter Randall-Page RA shows *Slip of the Lip* – a work of interlocking Hassan marble – the concept developed from drawings of eucalyptus seedpods. Higher in the garden is the work of other RA members – David Nash's *Black Mound* and Tim

Shaw's *Minotaur*. Billy Wynter's extraordinary *Camera Obscura* is carefully sited to give magical, internal views of the gardens. Elsewhere, visitors are drawn to work by Kishio Suga, Matt Chivers and Tony Lattimer.

A reconstructed Gold Medal show garden from the Chelsea Flower Show is also on the site. Darren Hawkes's 2015 Brewer Dolphin Garden impressed judges and visitors to the show with its 40,000 pieces of hand-cut Cornish

slate forming 'floating' platforms above ferns, aquilegia and dicentra. The garden's forms had been inspired by ancient dolmens and quoits, and featured an artificial underground stream. At Tremenheere, the garden has been reinvented, with the slate platforms overhanging a real stream, flowing through a series of ponds. Darren Hawkes is delighted. 'The space Neil had in mind… was exactly the sort of landscape which sparked my imagination in the first place; native planting of hawthorn and ash with that huge willow… I'm really pleased with how it looks in its permanent home.'

Neil and Jane have plans to further extend the site at its higher levels on its north-eastern side. With its world-class exhibits, it's already become one of Cornwall's most significant gardens. Along with the associated Tremenheere Kitchen, Artisan at Tremenheere, Tremenheere Nursery and Tremenheere Gallery, the garden hosts a series of special events throughout the year.

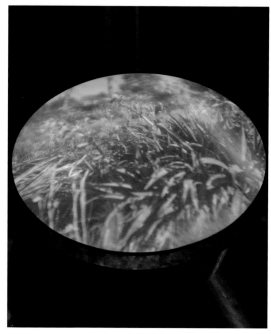

Top: Darren Hawkes's Brewer Dolphin Garden.

Above: Billy Wynter's Camera Obscura.

Trewidden Garden

Trewidden Garden lies in the far west of Cornwall, sheltered from the prevailing south-westerly winds by the Penwith moors and looking down over Mounts Bay towards St Michael's Mount. It's home to a variety of unusual, rare and exotic plants that thrive in its mild, maritime climate just a few miles from Land's End.

The land on which the garden now stands was bought around 1830 by Edward Bolitho, one of three brothers known as the 'Merchant Princes of Cornwall', who had made their fortunes in banking and the Cornish tin industry. Edward enlarged the house and extensive outbuildings, but it was his son, Thomas Bedford Bolitho, with his Head Gardener George Maddern and a team of some fifteen men, who drove the garden forward.

Away from Trewidden, Thomas Bedford was an important and powerful man, both in Cornwall and nationally. MP for St Ives, he was also a director of the Great Western Railway, owner of the Consolidated Tin Smelting Company, a director of Barclays Bank, and President of the Institute of Bankers.

At home, Thomas Bedford was a keen horticulturist, bringing the first *Dicksonia antarctica* to the garden. Taking personal charge, he planted the Tree Fern Dell, now one of the highlights for most garden visitors. An open-cast

Above: Thomas Bedford Bolitho.

Facing page: The Tree Fern Dell – one of the largest collections of Dicksonia antarctica *in the Northern hemisphere.*

Above: Magnolia sargentiana, *var.* robusta, *left, and* Gevuina avellana *(Chilean hazelnut), right.*

Facing page: The pond, developed by Thomas Bedford Bolitho, is today home to a sculpture – the Whale's Tail.

mine in Roman times, its ground was stabilized with rails from the family's mine to allow the initial planting of the ferns. It is now filled with specimens, including some of the originals supplied by Treseder's Nursery in 1902. Towering above are two Champion magnolias, *Magnolia dawsoniana* and *M. sargentiana,* var. *robusta*.

Thomas Bedford previously lived at Greenway on the River Dart in Devon (later the home of novelist Agatha Christie), which had a splendid garden in its own right. From there he transferred to Trewidden a specimen of *Gevuina avellana*, the Chilean

hazelnut, which was later described by the *The Gardeners' Chronicle* as 'probably equal to any other in the country'. He developed the pond, and constructed the two 'Curates' Vineyards', which, although needing restoration, are probably the only ones to have survived from the late Victorian era. Thomas Bedford died in 1915, but his widow lived at Trewidden until the 1930s.

Head Gardener George Maddern's son, George H. Maddern, followed in his father's footsteps as Head Gardener, and continued to build the garden's reputation as one of the most outstanding in Cornwall. John Crapp came to Trewidden around 1920 and became Head Gardener in 1930. He worked at the garden with his team of at least three – Arthur Manning, Sam Willis and Garden Boy Peter – until 1946, when he was succeeded by Harry Tully from Greenway.

In 1915, Trewidden became linked by marriage to what would become another of The Great Gardens of Cornwall. Thomas's daughter Mary married Charles Williams of Caerhays Castle (he was the son of the distinguished plant breeder J.C. Williams). She later became an accomplished gardener in her own right, and corresponded with the curators of the Royal Botanic Gardens at Kew and Edinburgh. *Camellia reticulata* 'Mary Williams' is named after her. After Charles's death in 1955, she moved back to Trewidden from Caerhays. Mary Williams was instrumental in refounding the Cornwall Garden Society and, at the age of 74, embarked on a tour of New Zealand and Australia to source new plants.

By this time the gardens covered some thirty-seven acres (15 ha), and included a south-facing walled kitchen garden. Glasshouses provided peaches and melons for the house. Ponds and fountains added interest alongside formal herbaceous borders seen against a backdrop of spring-flowering camellias and rhododendrons. A ha-ha gave uninterrupted views over Mounts Bay towards the Lizard peninsula in the distance.

During the Second World War, Trewidden House had been used as a Red Cross convalescent home and, each year, a reminder

Top: Head Gardener John Crapp.

Above: Mary Williams.

Facing page: Camellia reticulata *'Mary Williams'.*

of that time blooms in the garden. Springtime visitors are often surprised to see daffodils growing in the lawn by the pond in regimented rows rather than naturalistic clumps. These are the flowers of bulbs that were removed from the surrounding bulb fields to clear space for food crops during the war, and then replanted in the lawn by (perhaps rather unimaginative) land girls in straight lines, exactly as they had been growing in the fields!

Alverne Bolitho, Mary's cousin, has owned Trewidden since her death in 1977. He has been keen to carry on the tradition of improving the garden while respecting its historic legacy. It was he who took the decision to open the gardens to the public for the first time in 2002, working with Head Gardener Alison Clough, who started the restoration of the top section of the walled garden.

Now working with Alverne Bolitho is Head Gardener Richard Morton, who came to Trewidden in 2007. Born in Sussex, but growing up in Cornwall, Richard's first horticultural memory is as a boy helping his father dig out birch stumps in the family garden. 'It was my grandfather who was

my first horticultural inspiration, though,' says Richard. 'He was professionally trained and worked in municipal Parks and Gardens departments. I learned a lot from him.' Having worked and trained in Cornwall, Richard went on to study at the Royal Botanic Gardens, Kew, and came home to take up a Head Gardener's role in a private garden before moving to Trewidden.

Richard has been focusing on reclaiming parts of the original garden which had become overgrown. He has discovered some 'lost' rarities, and is identifying and accessioning the entire plant collection on to a plant database. The database lists over 300 cultivars of camellia, and is currently undergoing the registration process to become an International Camellia Society Garden of Excellence. Richard is proud of many of the specimen plants in the garden, but his particular passion is its collection of azaleas.

Trewidden holds the National Collection of Kurume azalea 'Wilson 50'. 'I'm in awe of Ernest Wilson,' says Richard. 'Just after the turn of the twentieth century – despite extremely difficult conditions – he managed to return from China with fifty varieties of azalea. The Royal Parks hold thirty-nine of them, and at the moment Trewidden holds thirty-two. One of my goals is to complete the collection of fifty here in the garden, to be the only one outside Japan. I'm excited by the prospect; I'm sure we can do it!'

Top: Alverne Bolitho.

Above: Head Gardener
Richard Morton.

Facing page: **Rhododendron**
'Tsuta-momiji' – Wilson 33.

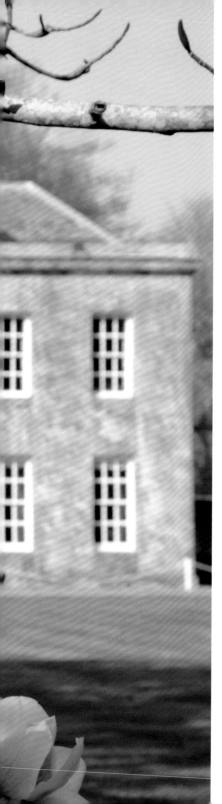

Trewithen

Michael Galsworthy has overseen a radical reworking of many parts of the garden.

Trewithen Estate, in mid-Cornwall, was a founding member of The Great Gardens of Cornwall. It is an International Camellia Society 'Garden of Excellence' – one of only fifty in the world – and holds twenty Champion trees (those that have been officially measured by the Tree Register and declared either the tallest or largest diameter of their type).

Although records are scarce, there is a likely mention in the Domesday Book of a house with land on the site of present-day Trewithen: 'The Count [Mortain] has one manor here called Trefitent... there is a half hide and it rendered geld for two ferlings.' Certainly by Elizabethan times it had become a well-established manor.

In the early 1700s, Courtney Williams, who was related to the Earl of Devon, built a substantial house on the site but became bankrupt. Some fifteen years later, Philip Hawkins, a wealthy attorney, landowner and MP for nearby Grampound, was the first member of that family to live at Trewithen. He commissioned London architect Thomas Edwards to rebuild the house in a Palladian style and to lay out the parkland. The house was constructed using granite from Hawkins' own quarry at Pentewan near St Austell. One of this granite's characteristics is that it contains a minute lichen, which

Specimen trees helped to create early vistas. George Johnstone introduced Rhododendron arboreum *and Trewithen-bred hybrids.*

shows pink when damp. The house seems to remain this colour for most of the year – testament, perhaps, to Cornwall's high levels of rainfall!

Philip died childless and Trewithen passed to his nephew, Thomas Hawkins, who retained Thomas Edwards' services for a few years. However, when he married, Sir Robert Taylor was brought in to redesign the house for the couple. The Hawkins family were well known as lawyers in London's Middle Temple, and Taylor was a fashionable choice who probably did much to increase the house's degree of sophistication to a level unusual in Cornwall at the time. Thomas Hawkins also had ambitions for the parkland and planted specimen trees (particularly oak and sycamore), creating the early vistas for which the house is still known. A notebook, written by him in 1745, on 'The Care and Cultivation of Trees' still survives.

Tragically, in 1766, Thomas Hawkins died after volunteering to have a smallpox vaccination as an example to his tenants. He was succeeded by his son, Christopher, who was keen to expand his estate so that ultimately he could ride 'from one side of Cornwall to the other without setting foot on another man's soil'. Well known in the county, he became High Sherriff, built Pentewan harbour, endowed local schools, was involved in clay, tin and copper mining, and became Richard Trevithick's patron, commissioning the first steam threshing machine from him. Significantly, Christopher Hawkins was also a founder member of the Royal Horticultural Society, and worked with two varieties of apple still grown today – Cornish Gillyflower, which he introduced, and Cornish Aromatic, which he made commercially available.

Rapid changes of ownership followed Sir Christopher's death, until George Horace Johnstone succeeded in 1904. He wrote:

> 'It was necessary to take an axe and claim air and light from amongst the trees, first for the house and those that should live in it, and then for the plants that must share the fortunes of the owner.'

However, George Johnstone was to do far more than clear trees. It was largely he who was responsible for developing the gardens as they are today. The South Lawn is maybe his greatest achievement at Trewithen. He used a Thomas Hawkins plan dating from 1725 to create the vista. Stretching for over 120 metres, it was originally planted with herbaceous borders; now both sides are planted with rare trees and shrubs. A clever use of perspective means that the eye is drawn to a focal point, beyond the lawn itself, at the end of the garden.

George also sponsored some of the great plant-hunting trips to the Himalayas and China, which gave him access to many of the new species that were exciting gardeners in the UK. The Camellia Walk at Trewithen is with flanked with plants grown from wild-collected seed, including *Camellia reticulata*. Another Walk in the current garden is named after George Johnstone. This has an example of what is now known as *Magnolia doltsopa* (Sweet michelia) – an extraordinary tree with scented flowers. It was introduced from the Himalayas by George Forrest in 1918. Also on the George Johnstone Walk is one of Trewithen's most famous plants, *Aextoxicon punctatum* (Olivillo), and a hedge of *Crinodendron hookerianum* (the Chilean Lantern Tree, named after Sir Joseph Hooker).

A major development in the garden was George Johnstone's introduction of dozens of *Rhododendron arboreum* hybrids. He also worked with Trewithen-bred hybrids (from *R. cinnabarinum*) – specifically 'Alison Johnstone' (named after his wife) and 'Jack

Top: Camellia reticulata *seed.*

Above: George Johnstone sponsored plant-hunting trips and developed the gardens as they are today.

Skilton' (after his Head Gardener, who was to go on to collect the Royal Horticultural Society's long-service medal, having spent all his working life at Trewithen). Magnolias were another favourite. Among many others, he planted a seedling of *Magnolia sprengeri* 'Diva', which had been given to him by his friend J.C. Williams of Caerhays Castle. George Johnstone wrote *Asiatic Magnolias in Cultivation* for the Royal Horticultural Society. Still a useful reference book, it was published in 1955, after which George Johnstone was awarded the RHS Royal Victoria Medal.

After his death in 1960, his daughter Elizabeth continued much of his botanical work, and was awarded the Bledisloe Gold Medal for Landowners, for services to agriculture and land management. In 1994, the estate was inherited by Elizabeth's nephew, Michael Galsworthy. Supported by Head Gardener Michael Taylor, and current Head Gardener Gary Long, Michael Galsworthy has overseen a radical reworking of many parts of the garden, including reducing and renewing the cherry laurel hedges.

Gary Long is also adding substantially to the plant collection by travelling overseas. He is Director of the International Camellia Society, and has visited China twice to see camellias growing in

Top: George Johnstone with his young grandson, Michael Galsworthy .

Above: Head Gardener Gary Long.

Facing page: The South Lawn, created by George Johnstone, is flanked with rare trees and shrubs.

the wild, and to bring back new plant material for the garden. 'The future plans for the garden are always in my mind,' says Gary. 'One big project is to develop a pinetum. We'll be working on ten acres (4 ha) of open farmland and planting an evergreen woodland so that visitors can enjoy a huge variety of conifers. In addition, we're working hard to restore parts of the original eighteenth-century water gardens.'

The garden currently holds twenty-four Champion trees. The rarest is probably *Berberis francisci-ferdinandii*. It's so scarce that it's only known in two other collections in the UK: at Kew Gardens and at Royal Botanic Garden Edinburgh. The plant was originally introduced to Trewithen in 1908, after its discovery for the West by Ernest Wilson in Sichuan, China. It had been unlabelled, and was growing, unknown, outside the kitchen. It was discovered (again!) by a visitor to the garden, Julian Harber, an expert in Chinese berberis. Together with Gary Long, he studied George Johnstone's records to confirm his find.

Trewithen is open each year from March to June.

Left: Camellia japonica 'Nuccio's Jewel'.

Right: Trewithen's rarest Champion tree is Berberis francisci-ferdinandii.

Facing page: Stewartia sinensis *is another Champion tree.*

Representatives of The Great Gardens of Cornwall, photographed in the Walled Garden at Trewithen, 2016.
Back row (left to right): Felicity Boucher, National Trust; Tom Henderson, Tregrehan; Charles Williams, Caer-
hays Castle and Gardens; Lorna Tremayne, The Lost Gardens of Heligan; Robert Dudley-Cooke, Lamorran House
Gardens; Mike Maunder, The Eden Project; Neil Armstrong, Tremenheere Sculpture Gardens. Front row (left to
right): Emma Evans, The Eden Project; James Humphreys, Trewithen; Gary Long, Trewithen; Richard Morton,
Trewidden Garden; Lucinda Rimmington, Caerhays Castle and Gardens; Nigel Burnett, Trebah Garden.

The Great Gardens of Cornwall
c/o Trewithen Gardens, Grampound Road,
Truro TR2 4DD, T: 01726 883647/883794
E: secretary@trewithengardens.co.uk
www.greatgardensofcornwall.co.uk

Abbey Garden, Tresco
Tresco, Isles of Scilly TR24 0QQ, T: 01720 424105
E: mikenelhams@tresco.co.uk
www.tresco.co.uk

Bonython Estate Gardens
Cury Cross Lanes, Helston TR12 7BA,
T: 01326 240550
E: sbonython@gmail.com
www.bonythonmanor.co.uk

Caerhays Castle and Gardens
Gorran, Saint Austell PL26 6LY, T: 01872 501310
E: enquiries@caerhays.co.uk
www.caerhays.co.uk

The Eden Project
Bodelva PL24 2SG, T: 01726 811911
www.edenproject.com

Lamorran House Gardens
Upper Castle Rd, St Mawes, Truro TR2 5BZ,
T: 01326 270800
E: info@lamorrangarden.co.uk
www.lamorrangarden.co.uk

The Lost Gardens of Heligan
Pentewan, Saint Austell PL26 6EN,
T: 01726 845100
E: info@heligan.com
www.heligan.com

The National Trust
Cornwall Office, Lanhydrock, Bodmin PL30 4DE,
T: 01208 74281
E: sw.customerenquiries@nationaltrust.org.uk
www.nationaltrust.org.uk

Antony
Torpoint PL11 2QA, T: 01752 812191
www.nationaltrust.org.uk/antony

Cotehele
St Dominick, Saltash PL12 6TA, T: 01579 351346
www.nationaltrust.org.uk/cotehele

Glendurgan
Mawnan Smith, Falmouth TR11 5JZ,
T: 01326 252020
www.nationaltrust.org.uk/glendurgan-garden

Godolphin
Godolphin Cross, Helston TR13 9RE,
T: 01736 763194
www.nationaltrust.org.uk/godolphin

Lanhydrock
Bodmin PL30 5AD, T: 01208 265950
www.nationaltrust.org.uk/lanhydrock

Trelissick
King Harry TR3 6QL, T: 01872 862090
www.nationaltrust.org.uk/trelissick

Trengwainton
Madron, Penzance TR20 8RZ, T: 01736 363148
www.nationaltrust.org.uk/trengwainton-garden

Trebah Garden
Mawnan Smith, Falmouth TR11 5JZ,
T: 01326 252200
E: mail@trebah-garden.co.uk
www.trebah-garden.co.uk

Tregothnan
St Michael Penkivel, Truro TR2 4AJ,
T: 01872 520000
E: enquiries@tregothnan.co.uk
www.tregothnan.co.uk

Tregrehan
Par PL24 2SJ, T: 01726 812438
www.tregrehangarden.uk

Tremenheere Sculpture Gardens
nr Gulval, Penzance TR20 8YL, T: 01736 448089
E: hello@tremenheere.co.uk
www.tremenheere.co.uk

Trewidden Garden
Buryas Bridge, Penzance TR20 8TT, T: 01736 351979
www.trewiddengarden.co.uk

Trewithen
Grampound Road, Truro TR2 4DD,
T: 01726 883647
E: secretary@trewithengardens.co.uk
www.trewithengardens.co.uk

We should like to thank the following for permission to reproduce photographs: Abbey Garden, Tresco, pages 12, 14, 18 (bottom); Abbey Garden, Tresco © Clive Nichols, pages 12–13, 15, 16, 17 (top), 18 (top), 19; Abbey Garden, Tresco/Eddie Rourke, page 17 (botom); Abbey Garden, Tresco © Howard Sooley, page 18 (bottom); Matt Biggs, page 8; Bonython Estate Gardens, pages 20–21, 22, 23, 24, 25, 26, 27; Fern Britton, page 8; Simon Burt/Apex Picture Desk, page 36; Caerhays Castle and Gardens, pages 28–9, 30, 32, 33 (bottom), 34, 35, 82; Caerhays Castle and Gardens/Charles Williams, pages 6, 33; The Eden Project, pages 40, 41 (bottom), 43; The Eden Project © Tom Griffiths Photography, page 39 (left); The Eden Project © Hufton+Crow, pages 38, 41 (top), 42; The Eden Project © Matt Jessop, page 39 (right); The Eden Project/Sophia Milligan, pages 36–7; Patrick Gale © Dan Hall, page 8; Jim Gardiner, page 7 (bottom); Tim Hubbard © Simon Burt Photography, back cover; Lamorran House Gardens, pages 44, 46, 48, 50, 51; Lamorran House Gardens © Marianne Majerus Garden Images, pages 44–5, 47, 49; Roy Lancaster, page 7 (top); The Lost Gardens of Heligan, pages 7 (background), 31, 53 (bottom), 54, 55, 56, 57, 58, 59 (top), 80, 82; The Lost Gardens of Heligan/David Hastilow, page 53 (top); The Lost Gardens of Heligan/Richard Stafford, page 59 (bottom); The Lost Gardens of Heligan © Heligan Gardens Ltd. Julian Stephens, pages 52–3; National Trust, page 66 (bottom); National Trust/Robert Morris, page 62 (top); National Trust Images/Andrew Butler, pages 8–9, 60–61, 64 (top), 66 (top), 67; National Trust Images/Carole Drake, page 63; National Trust Images/John Millar, pages 60, 62 (bottom), 65; National Trust Images/Juliet Turner, page 64 (bottom); Rick Stein © Anna McCarthy Press Center, page 9; Alan Titchmarsh, page 4; Trebah Garden, pages 70–71, 73 (bottom), 74 (top), 75; Trebah Garden © David Chapman, pages 68–9, 72 (bottom), 73 (top), front cover; Trebah Garden © David Chapman/Ardea.com, page 72 (top); Trebah Garden © Simon Burt, page 74 (bottom); Tregothnan, pages 76–7, 78, 80–81, 83 (top); Tregothnan/John Bradshaw, page 83 (bottom); Tregothnan/Christopher Jones, page 79; Tregrehan, pages 84–5, 86, 87, 88, 89, 90, 91; Tremenheere Sculpture Gardens, pages 92, 95; Tremenheere Sculpture Gardens/Neil Armstrong, pages 5, 96, 98 (bottom); Tremenheere Sculpture Gardens/Ali Braybrooks, page 99 (top); Tremenheere Sculpture Gardens/Mike Newman, pages 1, 10–11; Tremenheere Sculpture Gardens © Clive Nichols, pages 94, 97, 98 (top), 99 (bottom); Tremenheere Sculpture Gardens/Pat Wallace, pages 92–3; Trewidden Garden, pages 100–101, 102, 103, 104, 105, 106, 107; Trewithen, pages 108–9, 110, 111, 112–13, 114, 115, back cover; Trewithen/Michael Galsworthy, page 109; Christine Walkden, page 9. The photograph on page 116 is © The Great Gardens of Cornwall. Every care has been taken to trace copyright holders, and any omissions are regretted.

Special thanks to Lucinda Rimmington, James Stephens and Lorna Tremayne for sourcing the photographs.

The Great Gardens of Cornwall, 2017